Experiences in
Public Administration

Dennis R. Briscoe

University of San Diego

Gene S. Leonardson

Willamette University

Experiences in Public Administration

Duxbury Press

North Scituate, Massachusetts

Duxbury Press
A Division of Wadsworth, Inc.

©1980 by Wadsworth, Inc., Belmont, California 94002
All rights reserved. No part of this book may be re-
produced, stored in a retrieval system, or transcribed,
in any form or by any means, electronic, mechanical,
photocopying, recording, or otherwise, without the
prior written permission of the publisher, Duxbury
Press, a division of Wadsworth, Inc., North Scituate,
Massachusetts 02060.

Library of Congress Cataloging in Publication Data

Briscoe, Dennis R.   1945–
    Experiences in public administration.

    1. Public administration. 2. Role playing.
I. Leonardson, Gene S., joint author. II. Title.
JF1411.B74   350   79–23487
ISBN 0-87872-248-3

Printed in the United States of America
1   2   3   4   5   6   7   8   9 — 84   83   82   81   80

CONTENTS

Contents

Contents

PREFACE

Experiences in Public Administration provides instructors of public administration and public management with the first comprehensive set of exercises for experiential learning written at a consistent level and involving very small startup costs in terms of time required for learning the specifics of roles and the mechanics of the exercises. It provides new learning opportunities for students. It will help instructors guide students to an appreciation of the practical value of applying the concepts and theories of the field to the tasks they undertake as managers. In doing so it will enable and encourage students to continue to analyze and learn from their experiences when they function as managers.

The exercises in this book are not equivalent to the cases that are available both individually and as collected casebooks. Cases present real-world problems based on the actual experiences of public agencies and direct students to apply theory to the analysis of those problems. Students are then able to compare their analyses to the actions taken by the actual actors in the subject agency. Student participation in case learning tends to remain on a rather abstract level. In contrast to the case method, exercises require students to do role playing and simulate actual policy formulation and implementation and to use the tools of management. The impacts of personality and behavior, organizational structures and relationships, the environment, and other factors are demonstrated along with the use of particular concepts and management techniques in the practice of public administration. The use of exercises allows students to observe how their behavior, based on whatever set of assumptions and attitudes the students wish or are instructed to adopt, affects the behavior of other administrators and the outcomes of clearly defined situations.

The instructor using this book is able to direct the students' attention and learning to the particular concepts the instructor wishes to emphasize. Because the exercises are self-contained, they can be used in any order and in any number. They can be used to supplement a textbook. The instructor can assign the exercises in the order in which the theories and concepts they illustrate appear in the textbook. (Table 1, p. xi matches the exercises to the chapters of several introductory public administration textbooks.) The exercises can be used without a textbook for students who have already been introduced to the theories and concepts and are able to use them to analyze their experiences. Or they can be used by an instructor who prefers to teach concepts and theories without a textbook.

It follows that this book is appropriate for use in undergraduate and graduate courses and in training sessions for officials in government organizations. In each setting the instructor is able to lead the students to an understanding of the experiences provided by the exercises in terms of the breadth and depth of the students' understanding of the underlying theory and concepts. In turn, their appreciation for the value and their understanding of theories, concepts, and specific management tools will be advanced.

Experiences in Public Administration involves students in active learning—simulations, role playing, and problem solving—that requires the application of administrative theory and concepts and management techniques and tools to carefully defined problems of management. Participation in these exercises will enhance the ability of students to analyze and internalize the lessons of practical experience, providing them with an enhanced ability to learn from subsequent experience, a critical necessity in today's fast-changing administrative environment. In addition, comprehension and retention of theory and concepts are enhanced when students are required to use them for analyzing actual management problems and for solving real problems of administration.

Acknowledgments

The authors want to recognize the two experiential texts that gave them inspiration for many of the ideas and procedures used in this book. These two books are *Management: An Experiential Approach* (New York: McGraw-Hill, 1973) by H.K. Knudson, R.T. Woodworth, and C.H. Bell and *Experiences in Management and Organizational Behavior* (New York: John Wiley and Sons, 1975) by D.T. Hall, D.D. Bowen, R.J. Lewicki, and F.S. Hall. The authors also thank Dr. Gary W. Sorenson, Director of the Institute for Manpower Studies at Oregon State University, who provided the original opportunity to begin work on these exercises. In addition, the authors thank three reviewers: James Pfiffner, California State University, Fullerton; Kenneth Meier, University of Oklahoma; and David Paulsen, University of Nebraska.

Finally, the authors thank their wives, Georgia and Nancy, and their children, Forrest, Mark, Rebecca, and David, for allowing them the time and giving them the support that was necessary to finish this project.

TABLE 1. Relationship of Briscoe and Leonardson to Other Public Administration Texts

Exercise	Pursley and Snortland[a]	Starling[b]	Nigro and Nigro[c]	Berkley[d]	Henry[e]
1. Skills and Knowledge 2. of a Public Manager	1	1	1, 2	1, 2	1
3. Politics of Administration		2	2, 3, 11	2, 11, 13	10
4. Intergovernmental Relations	2	2, 3	9, 11	4, 13	11
5. Relations with the Environment		2, 3, 5	2, 3	11, 13	3
6. Administrative Responsibilities	3	4	6, 23, 24	12	2
7. Organizational Structure	4	7	7, 8	3	3
8. Organizational Design and Change	6	7, 8, 12	7, 8	4, 11	3, 4
9. Performance Appraisal		8, 13	18	5	6
10. Leadership	6	7, 12	11, 15	7	5
11. Employee Motivation	6	12	15	4	5
12. Intraagency Communications	6	7, 8	12	8	4
13. Planning/PERT	10	5, 6		11	6
14. Values and Decision Making		6	5, 11		5
15. In-Basket Exercise	11	2, 6, 9	11	7, 13	4
16. Evaluation	11	9	14	9, 11	9
17. Budget Allocations		3, 10	11, 21	11, 13	11
18. Types of Budgets	14	11	20	9	7
19. Affirmative Action	8	14	17	5	8
20. Negotiating a Contract	9	14	19	6	8
21. Careers in Public Administration					

[a]Pursley, R.D., and Snortland, N., *Managing Public Organizations* (North Scituate, Mass.: Duxbury Press, 1980).

[b]Starling, Grover, *Managing the Public Sector* (Homewood, Ill.: The Dorsey Press, 1977).

[c]Nigro, F.A., and Nigro, L.G., *Modern Public Administration*, 4th ed. (New York: Harper and Row, 1977).

[d]Berkley, G., *The Craft of Public Administration*, 2d ed. (Boston: Allyn and Bacon, 1978).

[e]Henry, N.L., *Public Administration and Public Affairs* (Englewood Cliffs, N.J.: Prentice-Hall, 1975).

Introduction

Introduction

Experiential Teaching: An Introduction for Teachers

These exercises apply behavioral science concepts to the practice of management in the public sector. The emphasis is on the practice aspects, although the introduction to each exercise relates concepts and theories to that exercise. It is assumed that the student is concurrently gaining a background of information about administration. These exercises are intended to provide practice in administrative techniques for those who already hold or are in training for management positions in the many different kinds of organizations in government.

The exercises have been designed for both new students of public administration and for the experienced practitioner and technician in the public sector. They were designed to integrate work-related experiences with formal class presentation of concepts of administration. Permanent learning needs to include both general concepts and active personal experiences and practice, both theories and action. Theories can provide general guides to action, but without an opportunity to test the theories in some form of action or practice, individuals will generally not integrate the theory into their behaviors.

These exercises were designed to require students to adopt the viewpoint of administrators: to pay particular attention to administrators' responsibilities, their relationships with the members of their organizations, and their performance of administrative functions. Most experiential material focuses on individuals and their interpersonal relationships. These exercises go beyond an interpersonal orientation and emphasize an administrative approach. Administrators, because of their responsibilities, perspectives, and opportunities for action in their organizations have distinct viewpoints. These exercises focus on the special significance of the administrative position. For example, while it is important for individuals to recognize the impact of their behavior on a group, it is critical that administrators do so. In addition, administrators must relate this impact to the goals of their organizations and to the numerous other factors which affect goal achievement. In order to emphasize this administrator's perspective, each exercise ends with the request that students summarize the learning experienced in the exercise both from their own individual viewpoints and from their viewpoints as practicing or potential administrators.

These exercises also examine the behavioral issues of administration. We feel that the behavioral aspects of administration are the most dynamic and the most difficult. It is in these areas that the most important problems lie and here

Portions of this introduction have been adapted from H.K. Knudson, R.T. Woodworth, and C.H. Bell, *Management: An Experiential Approach* (New York: McGraw-Hill, 1973), and D.T. Hall, D.D. Bowen, R.J. Lewicki, and F.S. Hall, *Experiences in Management and Organizational Behavior* (New York: John Wiley & Sons, 1975). Adapted by permission of McGraw-Hill Book Company and John Wiley & Sons, Inc.

that the capabilities and strengths of the administrator are most severely tested. Experience indicates that issues which involve interpersonal relationships or conflicting value judgments cause the most difficulty for administrators. The assembling of necessary resources or the analysis of technical reporting problems may be difficult, but it is usually the dynamics that go with implementing plans and proposals that are most trying. *Administration* has been defined as working effectively with people, and this is a reasonably accurate though simplistic definition. Working effectively with people is the heart of the implementation process.

Experiential teaching is teaching through experience, or through the use of exercises. It is teaching that emphasizes active practice of course concepts. It is, therefore, different from traditional methods of teaching. To aid teachers who choose to use these exercises, let us compare experiential teaching with traditional methodology in terms of the time required, involvement of the participants, control, flexibility, responsibility for implementation, and the amount and type of learning that takes place.

Like other teaching methods, experiential teaching provides participants with an opportunity to learn. What they do with this opportunity depends in large measure on their own motivations, their resources for learning, and the environment in which the opportunity is presented. But we have found that classes in which participants actively experience the course topics seem to generate greater involvement, continuing interest, and longer-term learning of useful skills than classes based on lecture or discussion.

It is important to recognize that the traditional relationship between teacher and student is not characteristic of experiential teaching. Much of the responsibility for the conduct of the exercises and for the actual learning itself lies with the students. This type of involvement generally creates great enthusiasm.

On the other hand, experiential teaching requires a lot of time for preparation by the teacher. It also requires that the teacher/trainer share much of the control of the learning situation with students and learn how to work in a less structured environment.

The role of the instructor in experiential teaching is very important. Rather than being a resource with guidelines, if not absolute answers, for the solution of problems, the instructor is responsible for focusing each student's learning and for creating an environment in which learning can take place. In addition to taking care of course mechanics that enable the exercises to go smoothly, the instructor must be a good observer of behavior, able to focus learning, clarify the processes, and assist the individual student or group in examining and analyzing exercises and their outcomes.

Under traditional methodology, students are expected to master a given body of conceptual material and to pass examinations on that material. In

3

contrast, in a system utilizing the experiential approach, it is expected that each individual involved will learn different things. We emphasize these differences by asking each student to reflect upon the exercises from an individual point of view: What did it mean to you? Subsequently, we focus on the ramifications of the exercises from the point of view of an administrator. At that point there should be more uniformity among responses, although there will still be some significant differences.

This focusing of attention on individual learning, rather than on the dynamics of the exercise itself, is very important to both the instructor and the participant. Each exercise requires participants to spend some time considering the learning acquired from the exercise. This is often difficult, for in a more traditional methodology this question is not raised, and students are often not prepared to deal with it.

Our own experience suggests that one of the most effective things instructors can do is to give the students supportive feedback on the basis of their review of these statements of learning. Because experiential learning is often a new experience for the student, supportive feedback is important. The absence of the traditional teacher-student relationship requires some adjustment on the part of both instructors and students. Support from instructors makes this adjustment less difficult.

The instructors also need to be facilitative. Groups often become involved in an exercise and desire more than the suggested time. Instructors should be more concerned with the learning than with the mechanics of the exercise or the completion of a certain number of exercises in a given number of hours. Instructors should be flexible enough to adjust their time schedules and plans when possible to meet the needs of their classes.

A collection of exercises such as this is based on a number of assumptions about learning in general and about experiential learning in particular. These assumptions, implied in the previous discussion, are as follows:

1. *Learning is more effective when it is an active rather than a passive process.* When a student can take a theory, concept, or practice and "try it on for size," he or she will be much better able to get a good fit, that is, an integration of the new idea with past learning.
2. *Problem-centered learning is longer lasting than theory-based learning.* If a person learns a new concept or theory only because it may be on an exam, there is little motivation to learn. On the other hand, when a person has a problem to solve and then scans for and applies knowledge which helps solve that problem, there is a greater likelihood of internal motivation to master that knowledge. For example, one of the authors took a number of statistics courses in college, covering analysis of variance in at least two of them, and

4

got good grades. He never really learned analysis of variance, though, until he had to use it, to apply it to a research problem.

3. *Two-way communication produces better learning than one-way communication.* This is more a principle of communication than an assumption. When a participant can interact with the instructor as well as other participants, information is likely to be communicated more accurately and the participant is likely to be more satisfied with the process. In such a situation, learning is more likely to be accurate and to generate involvement by the participants.

4. *Participants will learn more when they share control over and responsibility for the learning process than when the responsibility lies solely with the instructor.* When the instructor is the only one responsible for making the class "work," participants feel little motivation to make a success out of the learning process. When participants share responsibility for the class, more of their energy is likely to be directed toward making sure that the class is a success.

5. *Learning is more effective when thought and action are integrated.* Training designed to prepare people for particular forms of action (such as jobs in administration, personnel, and labor relations) should contain some form of action in order to get maximum transfer of learning to those future jobs.

The foregoing assumptions have important implications for the role of the participant and the role of the instructor. The key words in describing the two roles are:

Participant	*Instructor*
Sharing of responsibility	Sharing of responsibility
Examination of own experiences	Expert resource for content and for process
Autonomy	Guide, coach
Active involvement	Collaboration
	Flexibility, facilitation

In experiential learning, participants share responsibility for the learning process with the group leader. They are expected to observe, analyze, and learn from their experiences during the exercises. But they also have more autonomy than is usual in order for them to explore the meaning and personal relevance of the various ideas and techniques encountered.

Instructors or group leaders guide participants through the experiences and ideas they discover in the course and coach them on how to use the ideas to better understand themselves and administrative situations. Instructors may need to alter the course outline during the course in order to keep materials current with students' immediate needs or interests. This requires sensitivity to the class and a flexibility in providing experiences that are most appropriate at a particular time. In many ways, the instructor acts as a class quarterback in identifying useful ways to help the group get from here to there, but the whole team shares the effort, the responsibility, and the success.

Each of the following exercises has been written to be self-contained. Both students and teachers should be able to successfully complete the exercises by reading the included instructions. Exercise facilitators, class instructors, should thoroughly acquaint themselves with the exercise objectives and requirements ahead of time. It is then their responsibility to introduce each exercise, coordinate its activities, assign roles when necessary, and facilitate its successful completion. Of course, class leaders will also typically conduct the post-exercise discussion sessions and provide help and feedback on the individual post-exercise assessments of learning.

Experiential Learning: An Introduction for Students

The use of experiential exercises may be a new experience to both participants and instructors. You may be wondering just what experiential exercises involve. Participation in one or two exercises should provide much of the knowledge of how to learn from this kind of learning situation. Below are a few suggestions on how to make these learning experiences more effective.

1. *Get involved in the exercises.* Let yourself be free to do what the exercise asks you to do. If the exercise requires role playing, try to get into your role. If you are to analyze what's happening in the group, take a good look. These exercises will give you a chance to experiment with some new behaviors. The stakes aren't very high, certainly nothing like the risks involved in experimenting with new behaviors on a full-time job. The more you put into an exercise, the more you will get out of it.
2. *As you go through an exercise, consciously think about the relevant course readings.* The purpose of experiential exercises is to integrate theory and action. Each exercise is based upon some theory or concept in the field of administration. As you participate in an exercise, ask yourself: What concept or theory can help me here? What does this theory or concept tell me to do in this situation? What do my experiences with this exercise tell me about this theory or concept?
3. *At the end of each exercise, write down your own conclusions and reactions.* Think about what happened in the exercise and about how you can generalize from it. Ask yourself: "When might something like this happen again?" How and when can I use this learning again?" At first you may feel a little

strange writing down your reactions. As you get in the habit of doing it, however, several things may happen. First, you may find that you have drawn more conclusions than you realize. Second, you may discover that you have observed more than you are aware of. Third, your observations and conclusions may give you a sense of closure at the end of each session. And fourth, at the end of the course you will have a log of your own experiences and learning which can be impressive when you see them all together.

Writing down your reactions and conclusions can help close the learning cycle. Your learning cycle may work like this: An exercise gives you a chance to test out some ideas and concepts in new situations. In the exercise, you have some new experiences. Later in the exercise you examine what happened. Writing down what you have learned and your conclusions helps you form new concepts and generalizations, which completes the learning loop. This completion prepares you for more active experimentation based on your new concepts. To facilitate this process, a section called "Assessment of Learning" is provided at the end of each exercise for you to record your learning and conclusions.

Students-participants also have some different responsibilities under the experiential approach. Usually these responsibilities are new to students who may not be certain how to handle them. Unfortunately, the typical university classroom does not provide students with dynamic learning experiences that they control. Often it takes some time for students to realize that instructors using the experiential approach are serious about the whole thing—that they really intend to give much of the initiative and control to students. Once the barrier has been passed, however, students usually recognize that they can acquire a lot of learning for themselves and that it is mostly their responsibility to acquire it. Interestingly, the nonstudent practitioner who becomes involved in experiential learning seems to be more willing, even eager, to break from the traditional teaching-learning methodology.

Responsibilities of student participants include the usual preparation, such as outside reading. In addition, though, they must be willing to:

1. Become involved in the exercises.
2. Participate on a serious basis. Although the exercises are fun, the objective is learning. If the fun is overemphasized, learning will decrease.
3. Share ideas.
4. Analyze their behaviors and the behaviors of others.
5. Think about what is going on.
6. Help others to participate.

Although these requirements are easily stated, they are not met without some effort by individuals, groups, and instructors. In this regard, it is useful to periodically hold a "How-are-we-doing?" session to discuss how to make the group a more effective organization for learning. Such meetings are learning experiences in themselves. And they help utilize the potential of the collective talents of the class.

In summary, the exercises included here focus on the activities of administrators of public agencies. The exercises take place in many different types and levels of government organizations. They are designed to satisfy some of the training needs that continue to emerge in public administration. We are confident that this book helps satisfy those needs.

PART
I

Public
Administration

PART I Public Administration

This part introduces you to the scope of public administration, a multifaceted set of activities concerned with the accomplishment of government objectives. Public administration includes all the functions involved in the carrying out of the policies of elected officials. Many of the activities are found at all levels and in all functions of government. Because of the increasingly important role of government, the administration of public institutions is becoming one of the major management problems facing modern society.

There are a number of areas of competence that are important to all effective managers, including public managers. Managers must be aware of their political, social, and economic environments as well as have the skills necessary to both monitor and work within those environments. Only with adequate political, social, and economic skills can public administrators effectively contribute their own and their agencies' talents to the accomplishment of public goals.

Public officials are also involved in the process of making policy through their choices of alternative courses of action for carrying out policy and through their inputs into the policy-making process. Therefore public administrators need to be able to analyze and to make decisions about available alternatives for the accomplishment of public policies.

Public administrators must also be good managers. That is, after policies are decided, it is the public administrator's job to design the organizations, assign the work, monitor progress, maintain efficiency, and spend the money necessary to carry out those policies. These managerial tasks require the effective use of decision-making, systems and procedures analysis, and information systems tools. And they require extensive knowledge about how people behave in work organizations, since much of the work of a manager involves influencing others to act favorably toward the accomplishment of agency goals. This requires skills in motivation and leadership, effective interpersonal relationships with superiors and peers, organizational change, team building, and so forth.

Collectively, these points can be summarized by stating that the public administrator needs to develop the skills to manage the following sectors of government: environment, programs, finances, and people. Such an approach to public administration sees the public administrator as a professional, one who draws on the findings of many different sciences and other professions. The public manager with this type of professional approach is most likely to be effective in his or her meeting of public and governmental goals.

The exercises in this section indicate the variety of activities and influences which demand the time and complicate the lives of public administrators and make it difficult to pursue this professional role. The effects of the political environment on the performance of the public manager are emphasized. The exercises seek to demonstrate and develop the skills necessary for dealing with those effects. Later sections will focus on organizational and managerial tasks.

The first two exercises require students to demonstrate understanding of the scope and complexity of the field of public administration. Exercises 3 and 4 involve the most complicated and political task faced by public administrators: the distribution of limited resources among competing interests. A variety of techniques used in such situations are illustrated. Exercise 4 also demonstrates the important legislative/policy making role played by public administrators. Exercise 5 introduces students to the advantages, compromises, and pitfalls involved when a public agency cooperates with and avoids cooperation with other agencies. Exercise 6 explores the effects on public administrators of the concept of responsibility and of attempts to insure that the government remains responsible to its citizens.

SECTION
A

Introduction: The Skills and Knowledge of a Public Administrator

EXERCISE 1
Writing a Speech Describing Today's Public Administrator

Purpose

1. To introduce the roles and functions of public administration.
2. To introduce exercises as a way to learn.

Preparation

1. Read introduction to this part and section A.
2. Do step 1 of the procedure for this exercise.

Group Size

Any size.

Time Requirements

About ninety minutes.

Physical Setting

Movable chairs or facilities for small groups to meet without disturbing other groups.

Related Issues

The functions of management; the uses of managerial time.

A. Introduction

One of the frequent jobs of public administrators is giving speeches. In this exercise you are asked to assume the role of an urban planner in a Midwest city of about 200,000 people. You are the head of a planning section in the mayor's office. You are also president of the local chapter of the American Society of Public Administration (ASPA). In two months your chapter is sponsoring the regional meeting of ASPA, with the theme, "The Professional Public Administrator." As president, you will be giving the opening remarks. It will be your job to give the introductory charge to the conferees for the next few days. In your twenty-minute presentation, you want to outline the role of public administration as you see it today. You would like to paint an up-to-date picture so that the participants will have the proper focus for the rest of the conference.

B. Procedure

1. Prepare an outline for the speech. Include mention of the following points: the many functions and roles of professional public administrators; the challenges and changes you see occurring in the public environment that add to the demands on public administrators; the training that you see as necessary to prepare public administrators for this environment. Be as specific as you can in detailing your points. Rather than say public administrators must have political skills, indicate, for instance, that they must know how to work with citizen groups and must be able to interface smoothly with other governmental bodies. Prepare this outline prior to class.

2. Divide the class into five- or six-person groups. Separate the groups so that they can discuss without disturbing or being disturbed by the other groups (*five minutes*). Refer to appendix A for a discussion about the formation of the groups. Each group is to assume the role of a planning section headed by the person who is to be giving the speech. This person wants his or her remarks to discuss the various necessary roles of a public administrator today, with particular attention to how a professionally trained administrator would prepare for the challenges and changes that are foreseen for the 1980s. Of course, some of the speech will need to deal with what those challenges and changes are as well as why these particular skills will help a government manager cope effectively with the challenges and changes.

3. Each group is to prepare an outline of this speech, using the knowledge and experiences of all the members of the group. How you go about the process of putting together the talk from the members' already-prepared outlines is not as important as ensuring that all members have the opportunity to contribute. As the group outline

16

is developed, additional ideas and background will be brought forth that had not already been prepared. Each group should choose a spokesperson to present to the class (perhaps written on flip charts or a blackboard) the outline developed by the group. Since this is an introductory exercise, it is presumed that there will be a wide variance in the backgrounds reflected in the outlines (*thirty minutes*).

4. Each group (or a sample of them, if there are too many) is to present its outline to the class. This can be presented orally or in writing on blackboards, flip charts, or both (*twenty minutes*).

5. Debriefing and evaluation of exercise outcomes (*thirty minutes*).

C. Discussion and Conclusions

1. On which roles and functions of public administration did there appear to be a consensus? Why? Which other roles and functions were included? Do all of these give a clear picture of the job of a public administrator?

2. Which environments were mentioned as important? Was there anything left out? Why?

3. What skills and training were seen as necessary for public administrators? Why these? Would these skills adequately equip a public administrator to deal with the roles, functions, and environments that were mentioned? Do these suggest an emphasis for the rest of this course?

4. Did the class reach agreement on the functions and roles of a public administrator? Is such agreement likely?

5. What problems and challenges were mentioned? Why were these focused on? Does being able to recognize the problem areas and challenges guarantee they will be adequately dealt with? Why? Or why not?

6. How effectively did your group deal with this task? Why? What might you (as an individual and as a group) have done differently to make your group more effective? Does this point to skills which might be worked on during this course.

D. Assessment of Learning

Think about what you have done in this exercise. Try to identify two or three major points that you have learned from this experience. What meaning do these points have for you as an individual and for you as an administrator? How might you put this learning to use outside the class?

Consider only what you have really learned. Don't try to figure out what other participants say they learned, or what you think you should have learned. If you feel you didn't learn anything, think about why. What could you have done to get more out of the exercise? How might the exercise have been structured differently to provide a better learning experience? What could be done in later exercises to help make them better learning experiences?

E. Selected Readings

Gortner, H.F., *Administration in the Public Sector* (New York: John Wiley and Sons, 1977).

National Association of Schools of Public Affairs and Administration, *Guidelines and Standards for Professional Masters Degree Programs in Public Affairs/Public Administration* (Washington, D.C.: NASPAA, 1974).

Nigro, F.A., and L.G. Nigro, *Modern Public Administration*, 4th ed. (New York: Harper and Row, 1977).

Starling, G., *Managing the Public Sector* (Homewood, Ill.: The Dorsey Press, 1977).

EXERCISE 2
Hiring a City Manager

Purpose

1. To become acquainted with the job duties of a public official (city manager) in a public organization.
2. To gain experience in a major administrative activity, the interviewing and hiring process.
3. To begin thinking about administrative issues such as the description, measurement, and prediction of job performance.
4. To introduce the interaction of policy-setting bodies with the role of the administrator.

Preparation

Read the introduction to part I and the introduction to this exercise before class.

Group Size

A minimum of ten.

Time Requirement

A minimum of ninety minutes.

Physical Setting

Preferably a table or tables that can be used to simulate the setting for a group interview, with room for observers to remain unobtrusive.

Related Issues

Staffing, job design and selection, job hunting and interviewing.

19

A. Introduction

In this exercise you simulate the process of interviewing and hiring a city manager for a relatively small western college town. As you participate in this exercise, you will discover the duties and responsibilities of city managers, as well as their roles within a governmental organization. Three applicants for the job are interviewed by the city council and two employees of city government who have worked with the council to narrow the list of candidates. As the exercise proceeds, try to identify the combination of education, experience, knowledge, and personal characteristics which would be desirable for a prospective city manager applicant and how these would change as the nature of the city and its environment changes.

As broad guidelines for the concerns of the different groups in this exercise, the following categories of skills might be attributed to different levels of importance by various groups. In other words, different groups will want the new city manager to have different skills.

1. General management skills, abilities, experiences.
2. Specific job skills, abilities, experiences (budgeting, taxes, planning, program evaluation, legislative or policy body, public interest groups).
3. Technical information, knowledge, experience (for example, in different areas or levels of government such as health, utility services, transportation, public safety, education).
4. Specific job behaviors, ways of performing the job.
5. Political skills, experience, attitudes.
6. Plans and ideas for performance of this job and for this city government.

It should also be pointed out that any individual in this role will need to interact with many different types of people and groups. Some of these include, of course, employees; unions; users of the city's services, such as the elderly and building contractors; citizens, in general; the city council; other governmental bodies, such as the state and county governments and a loosely constructed local council of governments; the local college; and numerous local interest groups, such as the garden club, the area-development boosters (a group of businesspeople and developers), a strong PTA, and a strong local chapter of the Sierra Club. The importance of the candidates' attitudes toward and experiences with these various groups is, of course, a major consideration of the different people involved with the selection of a new city manager.

B. Procedure

1. Role assignments (*five minutes*)

    a. Three persons are chosen to be candidates for the city manager's position. See section F for general descriptions of the back-grounds of these three candidates.
    b. Five persons are chosen to be members of the city council who will be interviewing the candidates for city manager. See section F for general descriptions of the council members.
    c. Two persons will be chosen to be city employees who have worked with the city council during the selection process. See section F for a general description of these two roles.
    d. The remaining participants are to form small groups to deter-mine criteria for selecting among the candidates and to deter-mine how these criteria should be weighed. These groups are also to design a scale to use to evaluate the candidates as they observe the interviews by the city council. The criteria are not to be made known to the interviewers until after interviews have been completed. In small classes, this step can be eliminated or added to the activities of the city council or the two city employees.

2. All participants should read carefully the description of the city (section F) and be very familiar with their own roles. City manager candidates should prepare one-page résumés for the city council to read. The city council members and two city employees should prepare their interview strategy and prepare for the interview by discussing what they will be asking the candidates and what they need to know to make the final selection. The observers should prepare their criteria and weights for the selection (*twenty-five minutes*).
3. The candidates for city manager are interviewed by the city council. Candidates should not observe another interview until they have already been interviewed (*about ten minutes per interview*).
4. After the interviews are completed, each group (council, observers, candidates) should separately select one candidate and develop its reasons for its choice (*fifteen minutes*).
5. Groups should make known their choices as well as their rationales. The remainder of the time should be used for debriefing and discus-sion (*fifteen or so minutes*).

C.   Discussion and Conclusions

1.   What criteria were used by the different groups? Were they similar or different? Why? Was there agreement within the groups on what the criteria should be? Why? Did the members follow the criteria in making their observations during the interviews? Did they follow the criteria when making their final selection? Why? Were subjective and personal criteria used? Why weren't these made explicit?

2.   Is the interview a good way to gather information of this sort? What other alternatives are there? What deficiencies are there in the interview process? What procedures might have improved the results of the interview?

3.   Who was chosen? The person judged to be able to provide the best performance? Or the person judged to fit personally with those doing the selecting?

4.   How did the roles of the various individuals affect their decisions and behaviors? How can these types of differences be minimized? Should they be minimized? Why?

5.   Is the job of city manager any different than that of other public administrators? In what ways? Why?

6.   Could you now develop a job description for a city manager, including the following parts:
     - nature of the work
     - duties and responsibilities
     - ability, knowledge, skill requirements
     - employment qualifications

D.   Assessment of Learning

Think about what you have done in this exercise. Try to identify two or three major points that you have learned from this experience. What meaning do these points have for you as an individual and for you as an administrator? How might you put this learning to use outside the class?

Consider only what you have really learned. Don't try to figure out what other participants say they learned, or what you think you should have learned. If you feel you didn't learn anything, think about why. What could you have done to get more out of the exercise? How might the exercise have been structured differently to provide a better learning experience? What could be done in later exercises to help make them better learning experiences?

E.   Selected Readings

Refer to readings listed at the end of exercise 1.

F.   Participant Roles

City Manager Applicants

1. *Applicant 1*. Thirty-five years old. Masters degree in public administration with an undergraduate degree in computer science. Female. Two years as an assistant city manager in a larger city (90,000 population). Five years prior to that as a systems analyst in a large city. Two internships while going to school as an urban planner. Has worked closely in the past with citizen groups, trying to develop ways to use their input in city planning and zoning decisions.

2. *Applicant 2*. Thirty-two years old. Masters degree in business administration from a prestigious midwest university. Undergraduate degree in history. Male. For seven years has worked in rapidly increasing areas of responsibility for two electronics firms. Is currently regional director of Marketing for eleven western states. Previous assignment was as political liaison to federal and state govern-

ments for current employer. While going to school worked as a program evaluator in a Midwest county government. Has developed some environmental group interests, and has provided some legislative testimony for the Sierra Club on zoning issues. His career, though, has clearly taken precedence. He feels now is the time for him to move into the public sector, where he maintains his interests have always been.

3. *Applicant 3.* Forty-five years old. Bachelor's degree in liberal arts a number of years ago. Male. Until age thirty was a small businessman. Since that time, he has worked as either an elected official (school boards, water conservation districts, one term as a state legislator) or as a civic employee. He has held supervisory positions in small towns (two different ones) in both the operations and maintenance area and in the budgeting area. For the last three years he has been the city manager in a small farming community near this one (about 8,000 population). He feels it is time to move up in his career to a larger town.

City Council Members

1. *Small businessman* (retail store). Chairman of the city council. Member of council for ten years. Lifetime resident of state. Lived in this town for twenty years. Wants continued growth and development for town, but sees need to plan its direction.

2. *Local homemaker.* First term on council. Elected largely as a protest candidate. Has been very disturbed by what she views as lack of action by the council and by its seeming willingness to accede to wishes of groups she views as dangerous to the community. This includes the Sierra Club and student groups from the university.

3. *College student.* Political science major from the local university. Elected from the area in which student housing is located. Concerned about what he views as uncontrolled growth and lack of concern by the city for its large student population.

4. *Retired businessman.* Used to be an executive in a large forest-products firm. Has been on the council for three terms. Particularly concerned about the upgrading of city government to meet the growing demands on its services. Sees this as major roadblock to the continuing quality of life in this community.

5. *Teacher.* Engineering instructor from the local community college. First term on the council. Relative newcomer to the community (lived here for six years). Largely interested in learning and doing a good job as a council member. Very conscientious about role as council member. Wants to make sure council does

an effective job in providing guidance to the city administrators so that they can do their jobs. Sees the hiring of a new manager as an important step in this process.

City Employees

1. *Planner in the city manager's office.* Personally concerned with the style of the new manager. Think this has a big impact on the motivation of city employees to do a good job.

2. *Head, operations and maintenance section.* A long-term city employee. Very concerned about the practical experience of the new manager. Think a practical approach, backed up by first-hand experience, is crucial to understanding the problems of the different departments of city government.

City Description

The city is located in a western state and has an estimated population of 41,500. It lies about fifty miles from a larger population center of about 200,000 persons. The major employer in the city has always been the state college, which has about 12,000 students during the school year. There are also a couple of forest-products firms with about 300 employees each and an agricultural products cannery which only works at full capacity during the summer. Ten years ago a large electronics firm opened an assembly facility that now employs 1,500 people, including quite a few engineers and research personnel. The opening of this plant began an extensive area housing boom that is just now beginning to slow down. In the last two years there has been considerable growth in population, but much of it has been outside the city limits. Nevertheless, this has severely stretched the workload of many of the city's departments. And, obviously, this has created considerable upward pressure on the capacities of local merchants.

The city manager during this period of time resigned two months ago effective in two weeks. The council has narrowed its applicant list down to the three candidates that are going to be interviewed today. It intends to offer the job to one of these three candidates.

The following is a short outline of the services offered by city government:

1. Department of Human Services
   Social Services
   Health Services
   Health, Sanitation and Inspection

2. Department of Justice Services
   Police Department
   Court Services
   Corrections
3. Department of Environmental Services
   Planning and Development (zoning, planning, engineering services)
   Community Services (parks and recreation, permits, animal control, solid waste control, fire department)
   Operations and Maintenance (roads and bridge, fleet, sewer and water system)
4. Administrative Services
   Assessment and Taxation
   Public Elections
   Public Records
   Support Services
5. Office of the City Manager
   Administration and Planning
   Finances and Budgets
   Personnel and Labor Relations
   Intergovernmental Relations
   Data Processing
6. Special Bodies
   City Arts Commission
   Library Association
   Regional Council of Governments
   School District 12B

SECTION
B

Politics of Administration

EXERCISE 3

The Reduction of City Services: A Political Analysis

Purpose

1. To understand the concept of political resources.
2. To understand the political dilemmas inherent in reducing government spending.
3. To understand the difficulties inherent in trying to compare the political costs of alternative actions.
4. To experience the problems that accompany attempts to integrate analyses by several individuals of the important consequences of important actions into a single policy statement and to understand the sources of the differences in individuals' analyses.

Preparation

Complete step 1 before class.

Group Size

Any size.

Time Requirement

A minimum of one hour in class. Step 3 may be completed outside class if necessary.

Physical Setting

A room with movable tables and chairs in which groups of six or less students can meet together.

Related Issues

Budgeting, management of reductions in government services, problem solving, and decision making.

29

A. Introduction

Periodically, governments and government agencies face the necessity of getting along with less. Citizens may demand a reduction in taxes or tax rates, or refuse to approve levies for new services, or they may elect officials who are committed to reducing all government spending or particular programs. Struggles to maintain or increase budget levels or to minimize reductions place public administrators at the center of political activity. This exercise will sharpen your ability to analyze the political costs and benefits of administrative action.

You are the policy analyst in the office of the city manager of a city with a population of 250,000. In a recent election, four of the seven members of the city council were replaced by persons who are more fiscally conservative than their predecessors. The new conservatives have combined with one holdover in a coalition dedicated to reducing the city budget. Three members of the coalition are also social conservatives, in favor of reducing or eliminating most social welfare programs. The two members of the council who are not members of the coalition strongly support such programs. The two remaining coalition members cannot be classified as liberals or conservatives on the issue; they will support well-run social welfare programs that provide services of demonstrable need; they will not support others.

The city manager for whom you work is a political realist.* He defines his role as providing the council with information about programs and program needs that is as objective and politically neutral as possible. This information forms the basis for the council's decisions and helps in implementing the policies of the council in a manner that pleases the public. At the same time, he has been well trained as a manager and seeks to protect and foster the interests of the departments he oversees. He wants to avoid, if possible, the creation of a conflict situation in which individual departments attack each other in order to protect their own interests.

B. Procedure

Formulation of next year's budget has begun. It is clear that some budget cuts will occur. The city manager has asked you to prepare a confi-

---

*He realizes that retaining his job depends on maintaining good relations with the members of the city council, which in turn depends on the amount of public support for the council members which is generated by the provision of services for which he is responsible.

dential memo analyzing the political costs and comparative benefits of the following options: *

1. The current subsidy of the city bus system could be reduced. At present there is an innovative bus system that was established with an initial grant from the Department of Transportation but which is now maintained with city funds. The system includes a free zone in the downtown area. In addition, daily commuters to the downtown area are issued free monthly passes for the regular buses if they ride the bus at least half the time. A park-and-ride system provides express bus service from outlying areas at low monthly rates. Finally, school children and senior citizens are charged half fare. Any or all of these subsidies could be eliminated. Also, savings might be secured by reducing the number of runs; the buses run half-hourly during rush hours and are generally full, and those that run hourly during the middle of the day are frequently less than half full.

2. Financial support for neighborhood day care centers could be reduced or ended. The city government currently provides about 30 percent of the operating funds of ten centers located throughout the city. The remainder of the funds is provided by the local CETA consortium (40 percent) and by the United Way (30 percent). The centers were initially created because of the demands of several women's groups.

3. Library services could be curtailed. The main library is currently open sixty-four hours a week, the small branch library forty-eight hours a week. The bookmobile service to schools could be eliminated or curtailed. The practice of having at least one research librarian on duty during all working hours in each library has been questioned. Summer reading programs for children require two extra staff members.

4. The Fire Department, like its counterparts throughout the country, has by far the highest personnel costs in terms of productivity and hours actually worked. It has been estimated that the city's firefighters work an average of thirty minutes during each twenty-four-hour period for which they are paid. It has been suggested that at least twenty-five percent of the current force could be replaced by students from the local college who would perform fire fighting

*Your analysis is not concerned with dollars—how many can be saved by various options. You are concerned with *political* costs and benefits: What political resources will be expended, accrued, lost, or created? Who will be angered by the policy? How angry? How important (politically) are they? Who will support the policy? What kind of support? How important is that support?

31

duties during evening and nighttime hours in return for room and board at the firehouse. Volunteers might be used to replace still more of the regular force. Adoption of either or both of these ideas as policy would affect only the public relations activities of the Fire Department (visits to schools, rescuing cats from trees, and so forth).

5. The local free medical clinic receives 25 percent of its revenues from the city on a contract to provide specific services, including crisis and drug counseling and child health services. The clinic is perceived by many as a hippy support service and has been criticized in the press for poor management practices. However, there are no immediately apparent alternative providers of the same services. The clinic receives the balance of its support from the Community Action Program, the United Way, several churches, and a natural foods cooperative store.

6. Cuts could be made in or fees charged for the Parks and Recreation Department's full-year program of activities for children and adults. Programs are held in all the city's elementary schools and, for children, include at least two sports during each season of the school year and full-day programs during the summer. Programs for adults include folk dancing, handicrafts and hobbies, short courses on various topics, and supervision and coaching of the children's activities At present all of this is provided free of charge.

The steps for this procedure are as follows:

1. Prepare your memo before class after careful analysis of the options. The memo should explain the political costs and benefits of each of the options listed above and should then offer a set of recommendations on the options that the city manager could suggest to the city council. Bring the memo to class.
2. The class will meet as one or more group(s) of political advisors to the city manager. No group should contain more than six students. The group will seek to reach agreement on the relative merits of the various options and will develop a master list of recommendations based on that agreement.
3. Prepare a written analysis of the differences between your original memo and the group's analysis. What factors did you ignore? What factors that you feel are important did the group tend to deemphasize? How do you explain the differences?
4. Discussion (*a minimum of sixty minutes for all four steps*).

C.   Discussion and Conclusions

1.   What are the advantages and disadvantages of individual and group policymaking demonstrated by this exercise? How might a decision maker maximize the benefits and minimize the disadvantages of each while using both, as was done here?

2.   As a class, make a list of all of the political resources, costs, and benefits identified in this exercise.

D.   Assessment of Learning

Think about what you have done in this exercise. Try to identify two or three major points that you have learned from this experience. What meaning do these points have for you as an individual and for you as an administrator? How might you put this learning to use outside the class?

Consider only what you have really learned. Don't try to figure out what other participants say they learned, or what you think you should have learned. If you feel you didn't learn anything, think about why. What could you have done to get more out of the exercise? How might the exercise have been structured differently to provide a better learning experience? What could be done in later exercises to help make them better learning experiences?

E.   Selected Readings

Ilchman, Warren F., and Uphoff, Norma Thomas. *The Political Economy of Change* (Berkeley: University of California Press, 1969).

Starling, Grover, *Managing the Public Sector* (Homewood, Ill.:   The Dorsey Press, 1977), ch. 2, "The politics of administration."

33

SECTION C

Intergovernmental Relations

EXERCISE 4
Balance-of-State Advisory Council

Purpose

To experience group-based problems associated with resource allocation decisions: conflict, resistance to change, communication and leadership processes, and organizational politics.

Preparation

Read the introduction. For those not familiar with CETA, also read appendix C, "Background Information on CETA."

Group Size

Six (minimum).

Time Requirement

Two hours.

Physical Setting

Separate rooms for each group performing the exercise.

Related Issues

Group processes, power and authority, organizational structure, group roles, problem solving, and decision making.

A. Introduction

The governor has received supplemental CETA funds from the Department of Labor. The funds are earmarked for distribution for Title II B programs in the balance-of-state area. Of the total funds received, your planning district has been allocated $100,000 by the governor's employment and training staff.

You are a member or an alternate member of the employment and training advisory council for your local planning district. (You will be told which part you will play in a few minutes.) The council is made up of the following members:

1. Assistant manager of the region's largest town. The assistant city manager was elected chairperson of the employment and training advisory council by all the other members. The chairperson presides over meetings and votes only to break a tie.
2. Representative of the State Employment Service.
3. Representative of the local office of the Department of Vocational Rehabilitation.
4. Representative of the local Community Action Program.
5. Citizen representative from a disadvantaged background.

These are the only voting members of the advisory council. Note again that the chairperson does not vote except to break a tie.

Occasionally, one or more of the council members brings an alternate to the meetings. In such cases the alternate has the right to participate in the discussions, but may not vote.

Although the employment and training advisory council has no legal authority over the allocation of available funds and is charged only with giving advice to the prime sponsor (the governor) and the sponsor's staff, in reality the advice of the council is always accepted by the prime sponsor. Thus, the council makes the decisions that determine program design and the allocation of funds.

You were notified of the availability of the extra $100,000 at the same time you were informed of the time for the meeting that will allocate the funds among current program operators. The chairperson asked that each agency interested in receiving some or all of the funds submit the total requested prior to the meeting and to come to the meeting prepared to explain and defend its request. The following requests have been submitted:

> State Employment Service: $100,000
> Vocational Rehabilitation: $40,000
> Community Action Program: $70,000
> Little Tots Child Care Center: $5,000

You will be meeting with your alternate to prepare for the meeting. You will have fifteen minutes in which to develop your role and to discuss how you will defend your request for the extra funds. During this time you should do the following:

- Outline the arguments you will use to support your position at the council meeting.
- Determine the political resources you have available to help support your case.
- Decide what understandings, if any, you would like to establish with other council members before the meeting begins.

You may be as creative and as imaginative as you like in preparing the arguments you will use to support your position. Your imagination may extend to the creation of political resources.

The chairperson is committed to rational comprehensive planning and wants to see employment and training decisions based on rational rather than political criteria. The meeting, then, will run accordingly: the chairperson preferring decisions based on concensus reached by a rational analysis of alternative policies and programs.

B. Procedure

1. Role assignments and preparation for proposal defense (*fifteen minutes*).
2. Agency presentations of proposals (*twenty-five minutes*).
3. Council discussion of fund allocations (*twenty-five minutes*).
4. Agency caucuses and intergroup meetings to resolve conflicts (*fifteen minutes*).
5. Final council discussion and decision making (*fifteen minutes*).
6. Discussion and conclusions (*twenty-five minutes*).

C. Discussion and Conclusions

1. What decision-making procedures were used by the council? Why? What impact did those procedures have? What degree of ownership do the council participants have toward the final decision? Why?

2. What examples of "politicking" did you observe? What political resources did groups utilize? To what end? With what effect? How can an advisory council keep these kinds of behaviors from hindering the accomplishment of its goals?

3. What type of leadership was evident during the council meeting? Was it effective or ineffective? Why? What alternative styles could have been used? Why weren't they? Would they have been any more effective?

4. What did individual group members do to facilitate or block the making of these decisions? Why? What effect did those behaviors have?

D. Assessment of Learning

Think about what you have done in this exercise. Try to identify two or three major points that you have learned from this experience. What meaning do these points have for you as an individual and for you as an administrator? How might you put this learning to use outside the class?

Consider only what you have really learned. Don't try to figure out what other participants say they learned, or what you think you should have learned. If you feel you didn't learn anything, think about why. What could you have done to get more out of the exercise? How might the exercise have been structured differently to provide a better learning experience? What could be done in later exercises to help make them better learning experiences?

E. Selected Readings

Bailes, J.C., *Management Budgeting for CETA*, Papers in Manpower Studies and Education (Corvallis: Institute for Manpower Studies, Oregon State University, 1975).

Gortner, A.F., *Administration in the Public Sector* (New York: John Wiley and Sons, 1977).

Nigro, F.A., and Nigro, L.G., *Modern Public Administration* (New York: Harper and Row, 1977).

F. Participant Roles

Balance-of-State Advisory Council Roles

Assistant City Manager

Having recently received your M.A. in public planning and administration, you retain your belief that, with encouragement and the provision of the proper structure, the decisions of the employment and training advisory council can be made by concensus. You are sure that there is a best way to achieve any goal, and that with sufficient analysis of the costs and benefits associated with various programs and policies, all parties to a decision can be led to recognize the optimal decision. You also assume that once all parties recognize the best solution they will agree to it. Thus, you were delighted with your election as chairperson of the council; you feel that the position provides you with the opportunity to create an atmosphere and structure that will facilitate rational decision making.

You realize, however, that this afternoon's meeting is going to be a difficult one because the agencies represented on the board have requested more than the total amount of funds available. You want to encourage an open discussion and hope to avoid confrontation and bitter disagreement. You must decide how to go about achieving your goals.

Your position is complicated by the fact that the Little Tots Child Care Center has requested funds ($5,000) but will not be represented at the meeting. At the present time there is no administrator, and all employees are supervisors who work with the children. None of them is trained as an administrator; consequently, no one has been keeping adequate records or submitting the reports and forms required for the previous funding they have received. You are aware that they will not be able to continue receiving funds for very long if they do not begin to fulfill the administrative requirements that are attached to the grants they have already received. You believe that their program is excellent; it is also one of the very few available in the local area. It is important that the center continue in operation; therefore, it is important that they receive the $5,000 they have requested. Because one of their supervisors is ill, no one from their staff will be able to attend the meeting, and they have asked you to present their case for them. This you have agreed to do, although you are aware that chairmen are supposed to direct the discussion at the meeting, not participate in it, but you tend to become involved in

41

discussions of the issues you feel are important. Because of the small size of the council, this has never resulted in any complaints from other council members. Nevertheless, you try to limit your input.

You have been informed by the governor's employment and training staff that the meeting today must make a recommendation on the allocation of the available money. The money must be allocated to one or more program operator(s) before the close of business tomorrow. If the council fails to reach a decision, the governor's staff will make the decision for it, setting an unwelcomed precedent and perhaps causing the governor's staff to ask why the council was unable to act. Such an inquiry could lead to an investigation that might result in charges of conflict of interest against the program operators who currently sit on the board, something you all wish to avoid. It may be necessary to point this out to the other members of the board before the meeting today is concluded.

You need to think through what you want to achieve, how you will go about achieving it, what obstacles you will face, and how you will try to overcome those obstacles.

Remember that as chairperson you are responsible for seeing that the council meeting follows proper rules of procedure; that is, there must be a formal motion and a second before a vote can be taken, and so forth.

Representative of the Community Action Program

You are convinced that the employment service fails to serve the needs of the minorities, the chronically unemployed, the poor, and the others who are the special target groups of the Community Action Program. You also feel that employment and training programs should be directed primarily to serve these same groups. It is clear to you and to all others in your agency that the CAP is much better at providing to these groups the services funded by Title II B than are any of the old-line bureaucracies. Although you are willing to provide some funding to those bureaucracies to support the services they provide to other groups, you want to make sure that the majority of CETA funds are directed your way.

The CAP intends to use the funds it receives from this allocation to expand its activities in all program areas. The CAP subcontracts for the provision of some services, but feels that it is best able to administer the total range of relevant services when all funds are channeled through it. Given the political realities of the council, the CAP recognizes that it will never receive all available funds and is willing to bargain over their distribution. It likes to minimize all allocations to the employment service because of the conviction of the CAP staff that ES does not try particularly hard to find jobs for members of the groups which the CAP seeks to serve.

In planning your strategy and tactics for the meeting, you will want to be able to relate the purposes of the law (CETA) to the programs that you and your competitors offer to clients. You will also want to identify those persons in the community whose support for your programs you can cite. You must decide what compromises, if any, you are willing to make with other members of the council.

Citizen Representative

You are an activist. Coming from a disadvantaged background, you are convinced that the system is structured so that poor people can never overcome the disadvantages associated with their poverty. You are determined to help change the structure of the system itself and are an outspoken critic of the status quo.

You are convinced that the Employment Service is even worse than most old-line bureaucracies in its failure to try to help solve the problems of the poor. As a member of the advisory council, you remain committed to keep as much money as possible away from the Employment Service.

On the other hand, you regard the Community Action Program as the special advocate of the poor, the disadvantaged, and minorities. Your sister is on the board of directors of the CAP and you are very familiar with its capabilities and its programs and projects. In fact, you feel that the CAP staff is not a strong enough advocate for the CAP; you are convinced that staff members should participate in no compromises with other agencies. It makes you angry when the CAP's representative on the employment and training advisory council agrees to support the requests of the old-line bureaucracies for funds. Nevertheless, you have an intuitive understanding of the political process, of the need to win support by supporting others and engaging in compromise.

You must decide what arguments to make at the council meeting that will push the decision in the direction you want it to go. You need to determine the outside agencies and persons whose support you can cite for your position, and determine what aspects of the law (CETA or other) can be cited in support of your position. In other words, you must establish a strategy and tactics for your participation in the meeting.

Alternate Citizen Representative

As an alternate member of the advisory council, you are expected to attend council meetings and to vote when the regular citizen representative is not able to attend. When the regular representative is in attendance, you may also attend and participate in discussions, but you may not vote. The regular representative has asked you to attend today's meeting and to participate in the discussion, but he or she will also be in attendance and will be voting instead of you.

Like the regular citizen representative, you are from a disadvantaged background and feel that the system is structured so that poor people can never overcome the disadvantages associated with their poverty. You, too, are determined to help change the structure of the system itself and are a critic of the status quo. But you feel that the regular citizen representative is a bit of a hothead. You understand the need to compromise with the representatives and structures of the status quo and feel that through compromise you can help accomplish your goal of social change.

You look on the Community Action Program as the best vehicle within the existing structure for providing services to the poor and otherwise disadvantaged, largely because its board of directors and most of its staff are from disadvantaged,

43

poverty backgrounds. You would like to help direct as much money as possible to the CAP, but you also understand that the CAP will end up with no money in the long run if it alienates the old-line agencies.

You need to work together with the regular citizen representative in planning strategy and tactics for today's meeting. You need to help identify the best course of action to follow and the sources of support you can claim for that course, including legal provisions (CETA and other laws) and other available political resources. As a nonvoting member you may be able to facilitate compromise at the meeting, and this is one of your primary goals.

Representative of Vocational Rehabilitation

Your agency is badly in need of the $40,000 that it has requested. If it gets the money, it will use some of it to replace a badly needed therapist who recently had to be terminated because of the lack of funds available to the agency. The remainder will be used to expand a highly successful program for the physically handicapped which has had more than 90 percent of its graduates placed in permanent jobs over the past three years. Employers have been highly pleased with the graduates of the program and continually ask that it be expanded, but until this time there have been no funds available to carry out the expansion. You are convinced that no other agency could put the funds you have requested to better use and are determined to get them for Vocational Rehabilitation.

You will need to muster all the support you can. You should know what the law (CETA) says about prime sponsor use of your agency in the implementation of employment and training programs. You should know which agencies and officials who are not part of the advisory council support your agency and will support your present request for funds. Citing such support at the meeting may be helpful. Think through your strategy and as many tactics as you can before the meeting begins.

You will need to decide how you are going to deal with the other members of the council. It is your habit to cooperate with the representative of the Employment Service, largely because ES subcontracts for all vocational rehabilitation services it needs with your agency and because you are always able to reach an understanding more easily with their representative than with other members of the council. ES recognizes the value of continuing old-line programs such as yours, and you have express instructions from your superiors not to alienate the ES representative during your service on the council.

Representative of the Employment Service

You share your agency's conviction that the Employment Service is capable of providing or subcontracting to provide all employment and training services, and you regard any allocations of employment and training funds made directly to other agencies as an encroachment on your turf. You recognize that other old-line agencies, such as Vocational Rehabilitation and Vocational Education, are the appropriate subcontractors for the provision of the services in which they specialize, but basically you feel that the Employment Service ought to administer all funds and subcontract with other specialized agencies. Nevertheless, you recognize the political necessity of having allies on the employment and training advisory council and from time to time are willing to support the request of other agencies for direct funding. In this particular case, your superiors in the Employment Service have expressed their desire for you to obtain all of the available $100,000, and you have turned in a request to that effect. Inflation has cut seriously into the ES budget and these funds are needed to bring back staff members who have had to be laid off in the last month. Of course you cannot justify your request on that basis. You plan to justify your request by claiming that the funds will be used to hire two badly needed job developers, to subcontract for a very appealing institutional training program designed by the local community college, and to vastly improve the local labor market data base and analysis through the purchase of some computer software which will support the activities of an expert labor market statistician who recently has been hired by your agency. You must decide whether you will bargain for the support of one or more other members of the council in return for your support of their position now or in the future.

As you develop your strategy and tactics, you need to identify persons outside the advisory council whose support you can cite in arguing for the appropriation you desire. You will want to know what the law (CETA) says about prime sponsor utilization of the Employment Service. Any outside support you can cite on your behalf may be helpful.

SECTION
D

Relations With the Environment

EXERCISE 5

The Veterans' Action Committee's Drug Abuse Center

Purpose

1. To experience the potential gains and frustrations associated with one agency's voluntary and required interactions with other agencies in its environment.
2. To demonstrate the problems of communication related to those interactions.
3. To experience the problems and procedures associated with the pursuit of federal grants.

Preparation

Read the introduction and procedure. Complete steps 1 to 6 of the procedure before class. The instructor will inform the students whether step 5 will be carried out.

Group Size

Minimum of ten (two assigned to each organization) plus the course instructor, who plays the role of the A-95 coordinator. A class of more than twenty students may be divided into two separate simulations, but a teaching assistant or other instructor would be required for the role of A-95 coordinator if the groups were to meet at the same time.

Time Requirement

Minimum of ninety minutes, with considerable additional out-of-class work.

Physical Setting

A seminar room or other facility in which a roundtable discussion is possible will be helpful but not essential. Separate rooms will be necessary if more than one group performs step 7 at the same time.

49

Related Issues

Group processes, intergovernmental relations, decision making, power, grant writing.

A. Introduction

Earlier exercises dealing with the politics of administration and intergovernmental relations have illustrated the importance of an organization's relations with its environment. One means by which an organization may develop positive support or neutrality among other, potentially rival, organizations is examined here. Specifically, this exercise demonstrated the role which communication can play in avoiding confrontations over turf — an example of the role that communication can play in avoiding other confrontations as well.

During the exercise you will be involved in a simulation of the A-95 process. This process, created by the federal government's Office of Management and Budget (OMB), provides for the review of one agency's proposal for a national grant by other state and local agencies whose activities are related to those suggested in the grant proposal. The review is conducted by A-95 clearinghouses that exist at both state and local levels. Regulations governing the application process for a particular grant will specify if an application must be submitted to the clearinghouse. If it must, it will be submitted to a local clearinghouse if the proposed activity will be confined to a single locality, or to the statewide clearinghouse if it will affect a broader area. The clearinghouse, often only a single person (the A-95 coordinator), reads the proposal and determines which other agencies have an interest in the proposed program or activity, then sends the proposal to those agencies for their review and comment. Those agencies have thirty days in which to indicate whether they wish to comment; if they do, they are given additional time. If no comments are received, the proposal is returned with clearinghouse clearance to the agency that wrote it. If comments are received and no consensus is apparent, the clearinghouse may arrange a meeting to attempt to achieve some agreement on the proposal. With or without agreement, the proposal is eventually sent on to the funding agency along with all the comments and the recommendation of the clearinghouse. The funding agency is not required to accept any of the recommendations and may fund a proposal that has received all negative comments and a negative recommendation from the clearinghouse.

The U.S. Department of Health, Education and Welfare (HEW) has recently instituted a grant program that makes funds available for the creation and implementation of drug abuse programs that will serve segments of the population that do not receive adequate service from existing programs. Funding decisions are made on a case-by-case basis in HEW's offices in Washington, D.C.; proposals are subject to A-95 review.

A group of Vietnam veterans in a small town—the Veterans' Action Committee—hears about and decides to apply for program funds. The veterans involve two other agencies in their proposal writing. Those two agencies and two others are subsequently asked to comment on the proposal. The A-95 clearinghouse for the area decides to schedule a meeting of all the commenting agencies so that each may hear the comments of the others.

Students in this exercise will be divided into groups representing each of the five agencies. The instructor will play the role of the A-95 coordinator. The assignment of roles and the meeting of the A-95 clearinghouse and subsequent discussion (steps 1, 8, and 9) will be done in class. The instructor will decide which, if any, of the other steps will be completed during class time and establish deadlines for the completion of each step.

B. Procedure

1. Role assignment. Role descriptions appear at the end in section F (*five minutes*).
2. The Veterans' Action Committee meets to establish goals and objectives and to prepare the preliminary discussion paper. It then arranges for the meeting described in step 3 (*one hour*).
3. The Veterans' Action Committee meets with the representatives of the doctors' clinic and the state's mental health division to obtain their help and advice for the preparation of the grant proposal. The entire group writes as much of the proposal as it can agree on (*two hour maximum*).
4. The Veterans' Action Committee completes its proposal and submits it to the A-95 coordinator (the instructor) (*one hour maximum*).
5. The A-95 coordinator gives copies of the proposal to the representatives of the doctors' clinic, the Psychological Counseling Service, Inc., the veterans' hospital, and the state's mental health division for their review and sets a deadline for the submission of the written comments and a date for the meeting of the clearinghouse that will review the proposal and comments (*in class or outside class*).

51

6. The four agencies prepare their written comments, using the A-95 comment form given at the end of this exercise, and submit them to the A-95 coordinator. It is anticipated that the two agencies which had no part in writing the proposal will spend a great deal more time on this step than will the other two agencies.

7. The A-95 coordinator reviews the written comments and prepares comments and questions for the meeting of the clearinghouse.

8. The clearinghouse meets. With the coordinator running the meeting, each agency reviews its comments, and the discussion seeks to overcome any disagreements and define a proposal that could be supported by all. Success may not be achieved; the objective is to illustrate the scope of the problem (*fifty minutes*).

9. Discussion and conclusions (*forty minutes*).

C. Discussion and Conclusions

1. Analyze the differences in the responses of the different organizations to the proposal. In what ways did the responses differ? Why did they differ? What differences, if any, in the responses can be attributed to involvement in the initial writing of the proposal (that is, if they differed, why did the response of the doctors' clinic differ from that of the Psychological Counseling Service and that of the mental health division differ from that of the veterans' hospital)?

2. How many effective ways for an organization to deal with potential or actual opposition in the environment can you identify? Explain their strengths and weaknesses.

3. What is the importance of information as a political resource? How does the need to communicate, demonstrated in this exercise, relate to the need to use information as a political resource?

4. How well would you expect the A-95 process to work in the real world of organizational politics? Why? (The instructor should describe briefly the past record of the process.)

D. Assessment of Learning

Think about what you have done in this exercise. Try to identify two or three major points that you have learned from this experience. What meaning do these points have for you as an individual and for you as an administrator? How might you put this learning to use outside the class?

Consider only what you have really learned. Don't try to figure out what other participants say they learned, or what you think you should have learned. If you feel you didn't learn anything, think about why. What could you have done to get more out of the exercise? How might the exercise have been structured differently to provide a better learning experience? What could be done in later exercises to help make them better learning experiences?

E. Selected Readings

1. Hall, M., *Developing Skills in Proposal Writing*, Second Edition (Portland, Oregon: Continuing Education Publications, 1977).
   Intergovernmental Relations and Regional Operations Division of the Office of Management and Budget, *A-95: What It Is—How It Works* (Washington, D.C.: Government Printing Office, July 1, 1976).
3. Pursley, R.D. and Snortland, N., *Managing Government Organizations* (North Scituate, Mass.: Duxbury Press, 1980), chapter 2.
4. Selznick, P., *TVA and the Grassroots* (Berkeley and Los Angeles: University of California Press, 1949).
5. Simmons, R.H. and Dvorin, E.P., *Public Administration: Values, Policy, and Change* (Port Washington, N.Y.: Alfred Publishing Co., 1977).

F. Participant Roles

The Veterans' Action Committee

You are the organizers of the Veterans' Action Committee, a group which has come together in a rather casual fashion with the goal of helping veterans from Vietnam deal with the problems of integrating their lives into a small-town community. The group began simply; you and several friends decided that you would enjoy knowing and helping other veterans. At first the only activities were rapping and beer drinking, but the frustrations which various individuals felt in dealing with their reentry into society soon produced various organized activities. The most important of these has been an employment program that has sought to use the Employment Service, local CETA and public works programs, and direct appeals to area employers to find jobs for unemployed veterans. Other activities have been more social in nature, including the organization of sports teams to participate in local leagues.

The employment program has been rather successful, but your good intentions have occasionally been frustrated by the poor job performance of individual veterans. In almost all cases, this poor performance is related to problems of drug abuse. You have become convinced that the greatest service you could perform for your peers would be to help them overcome problems associated with drug abuse. Consequently you are determined to institute a drug counseling program and, if possible, to open a drug abuse center for veterans. You are convinced that your good will, empathy, and identity as veterans will enable you to perform such a service; your other self-help groups have had good success.

You have heard from friends in another town about a grant program through which the U.S. Department of Health, Education and Welfare (HEW) provides funds for drug abuse programs. Checking with HEW, you learn that up to $65,000 a year could be available for such a program in your town. Although the funds are not earmarked for veterans, they can be used for such a specialized service. You decide to submit a grant proposal for the funds.

You are fully aware of your lack of expertise and credentials, although you are confident that rap sessions and other forms of mutual support involving two or more veterans can help most individuals overcome their drug-related problems. You recognize your need for help in proposal writing and in designing a program acceptable to HEW. You have no idea how you would spend $65,000 on such a program, but it has occurred to you that several unemployed veterans might be able to find work with the program. You ask the local doctors' clinic and the office of the state's mental health division located in a nearby city to help you write the proposal. They agree to help.

Early in your discussions with HEW you discover that your proposal will have to undergo A-95 review, a procedure which enables other agencies involved in running similar programs in the same geographic area to comment on your proposal, particularly on whether it duplicates or conflicts with other services available in that same area. With $65,000 and the local turf at stake, this reinforces your conviction that you must write a good proposal in order to receive any funds.

54

Your first task is to prepare for the meeting with those two agencies. You must prepare a draft proposal as a basis for discussion; in it you should define the problem, your approach to solving the problem, the target population, a preliminary budget, a staffing and administrative plan, and so on. In other words, you should define your goals and objectives and your approach to achieving those goals and objectives. You should present this initial draft to the other two groups as a discussion paper only and ask for their help in refining it into a viable proposal. It is important to know that both of them are likely to be invited by the A-95 clearinghouse to comment on your proposal.

Once you have prepared your draft proposal, meet with the other two agencies. After that meeting, you must decide what to do with the suggestions and demands of those agencies. Then write your final proposal and submit it to the A-95 clearinghouse for review. The clearinghouse coordinator will submit your proposal to other agencies for comments and then call a meeting to review the proposal and the written comments it receives. The meeting is held in order to enable the coordinator to understand all of the issues and arguments before making a recommendation to HEW on whether to fund the program you propose.

The Doctors' Clinic's Planning Staff

You are the planning staff of the doctors' clinic located in the same town as the Veterans' Action Committee. The clinic was established by a small group of doctors who were concerned about the lack of good medical services in nonurban areas and who wanted to live in such an area as well. You are among those doctors who helped establish the clinic and you continue to place heavy emphasis on the provision to the community of quality medical service by well-trained personnel. For some time you have been concerned about the lack of efficient counseling services for the community and have been seeking ways to increase the number of competent psychologists and counselors in town.

The veterans' group, recognizing your commitment to community welfare and your expertise, invite you to help prepare its grant proposal. You are curious and hopeful that a good program can be devised, but also worried about the quality of the services the group would provide with such a grant. For these reasons, you agree to try to help them.

You will attend a planning session with the Veterans' Action Committee; the state's mental health division will also be represented at the meeting. You will be there in response to the veterans' request for help. You will have to decide how much help you are willing to give.

Once the proposal has been completed and submitted to the A-95 clearinghouse, it will be returned to you by the clearinghouse for your comments. You will be asked to recommend funding or nonfunding. The clearinghouse will forward your comments, along with all others, to HEW, which will make the final decision on whether to fund the proposal. Complete the A-95 response form and prepare any additional written commentary that will support or explain your position. Be prepared to defend your position orally at the meeting of the A-95 clearinghouse.

Local Office, State Mental Health Division

You are the director and assistant directors of an office of the state's mental health division. You are all psychologists, but most of the rest of your staff is made up of counselors. Your office is located in a large city whose periphery is just thirty miles from the town in which the Veterans' Action Committee wants to establish a drug counseling service.

Because of your expertise and your political connections, the veterans' group has asked you to help prepare its grant proposal. You find the idea of providing drug counseling to veterans a good one and recognize that currently it is not being done, but you are concerned because the veterans making the proposal have no expertise or credentials to qualify them to carry out such a program. As the state's agency responsible for the provision of such services, you welcome the opportunity to participate in their planning and hope to help shape a viable program for the proposal if you decide to support the proposal.

Your superiors in the state capital would like you to develop such a program, and many other new programs, in your area. They are ambitious and want the division to grow. However, the current political climate—the frugal attitudes of taxpayers—suggests the folly of duplicating services and the wisdom of avoiding the administrative costs incurred by running outpatient programs in locations removed from your city.

You will attend a planning session with the Veterans' Action Committee; the town's doctors' clinic will also be represented at the meeting. You will be there in response to the veterans' request for help. You will have to decide how much help you are willing to give.

Once the proposal has been completed, it will be returned to you by the A-95 clearinghouse for your comments. You will be asked to recommend funding or non-funding. The clearinghouse will forward your comments, along with all others, to HEW, which will make the final decision on whether to fund the proposal. Complete the A-95 response form and prepare any additional written commentary that will support or explain your position. Be prepared to defend your position orally at the meeting of the A-95 clearinghouse.

Psychological Counseling Service, Inc.

You comprise the board of directors of the Psychological Counseling Service, Inc., a local group of professionals (three psychologists, four counselors) that is supported by several federal and state grants. Your offices are in the same town as the Veterans' Action Committee. You already have grants for the provision of counseling services relating to family problems, teenage drinking and drug problems, and suicide crises. You also provide numerous other counseling services that are not directly supported with grant funds.

You are committed to serving those in need and to charging patients only what they can afford. You rely on your grants to cover most administrative costs, and you view the securing of additional grants as bascially important to the maintenance of quality in your program and the achievement of broad coverage in the community.

This new grant for the provision of doing counseling would be ideally suited to support the purposes and activities of your organization. You are surprised that you weren't aware of its availability until you received the invitation from the A-95 clearinghouse to comment on the veterans' organization's proposal. You recognize that the awarding of such a grant to that organization would prevent your organization from receiving one.

Your job now is to evaluate the proposal and recommend funding or nonfunding to the A-95 clearinghouse. The clearinghouse will forward your comments, along with all others, to HEW, which will make the final decision on whether to fund the proposal. Without consulting the veterans' organization, complete the A-95 response form and prepare any additional written commentary that will support or explain your position. Be prepared to defend your position orally at the meeting of the A-95 clearinghouse.

Veterans Hospital Planning Staff

Although planning is not the primary responsibility of any of you, you are the planning staff for a veterans hospital located only thirty miles from the town where the Veterans' Action Committee wants to establish its drug counseling service. Your hospital is situated on the edge of a large city. There are three other hospitals in the city, and together the four hospitals are competent to handle any and all medical problems. Your hospital has not developed an in-house program aimed specifically at drug abuse, but your counselors are well equipped in training and experience to deal with such problems and are willing to refer difficult cases to specialists within the city. Of course the Veterans Administration pays for all such treatment, so such referrals do not place financial burdens on the patients involved.

More than a year ago the hospital's directors had asked you to develop a plan for the delivery of drug counseling services in the hospital. It is clear that the doctors want such a service housed within the hospital. However, you have failed to identify a means for the delivery of such services that would not be very expensive— too expensive to justify the program. You had not heard about the new grant program which is the subject of this proposal until you received the proposal from the A-95 clearinghouse.

Concerned with the constantly rising costs of medical care, you oppose unnecessary duplication of services. You also recognize the wisdom of providing outpatient services where they are needed rather than requiring all patients to come to the hospital. Your hospital is responsible for the provision of services to a very large geographic area, much larger than that which will be covered by the program described in this proposal. Among those services which it is required to provide directly or through some other agency or agencies are the drug counseling services that this proposal seeks to establish.

Your job now is to evaluate the proposal and recommend funding or nonfunding to the A-95 clearinghouse. The clearinghouse will forward your comments, along with all others, to HEW, which will make the final decision on whether to fund the proposal. Keeping in mind your various responsibilities and the desires of your board of directors, complete the A-95 response form and prepare any additional written commentary that will support or explain your position. Be prepared to defend your position orally at the meeting of the A-95 clearinghouse.

A-95 Clearinghouse
Proposal Comment Form

The A-95 clearinghouse has received a grant proposal to be submitted by the <u>Veterans' Action Committee</u> to <u>HEW</u> for funds to be used for the following purpose(s): <u>to establish a</u> <u>Drug Abuse Center for veterans.</u>

_____

_____.

A copy of the grant proposal is attached. Please submit your written comments regarding the proposal to the A-95 coordinator no later than _____.

In your comments, please answer the following questions:

1. Does the proposed activity duplicate a current activity of your organization or of some other organization with which you are familiar? If it is duplicative of an existing activity, is there sufficient need for the additional activity to justify the funding of its duplication as proposed?
2. Does the proposed activity duplicate an activity which your agency plans to undertake in the future? If so, how do your budget projections for the activity compare with those presented in this proposal?
3. Does the proposed activity conflict with any current or planned activity of your organization or of any other organization with which you are familiar? If so, what is the nature of the conflict? Can the conflict be resolved? How?
4. How would you assess the proposed activity in terms of its likely cost effectiveness? If you feel the fund request is too high, by how much would you reduce it? Please explain why your suggested budget- and activity-level proposals would be more cost effective than those in this proposal.
5. What suggestions do you have for the improvement of the proposal?
6. Do you recommend funding the proposed activity, rewriting the proposal, or not funding the proposal?

SECTION
E

Administrative Responsibility

EXERCISE 6

Administrative Responsibility: Problems and Control Mechanisms

Purpose

1. To examine and develop an appreciation for aspects of public administrative responsibility.
2. To compare aspects of administrative responsibility with pitfalls and barriers to such responsibility.
3. To develop an understanding of problems of responsibility at different levels of government.

Preparation

Read the introduction.

Group Size

Any size, broken into groups of five to seven members.

Time Requirement

Ninety minutes.

Physical Setting

Movable chairs or facilities for small groups to meet without disturbing other groups.

Related Issues

External relations, intergovernmental relations, communications.

63

A. Introduction

One of the major influences on the attitudes and behaviors of public administrators is the set of values and standards that the public expresses toward what could be labeled "administrative responsibility" or "social responsibility."* In the 1970s and 1980s there has been increasing public and media attention paid to governmental responsibility in terms of criteria such as:

1. Responsiveness to public needs and interest
2. Flexibility in meeting the changing needs
3. Consistency in approach to various interest groups
4. Stability and predictability in the provision of services
5. Legality and prudence in actions.
6. Honesty and openness in decision making and public pronouncements.
7. Accountability of individuals and programs for results
8. Competency in trying to accomplish public goals.
9. The provision of due process for constituents who have grievances against the system

Of course, a number of barriers have always arisen to the effective expression of administrative responsibility by public managers. These pitfalls and barriers have included problems with political favoritism, nepotism, coercion of dissenters, collusion of government with special interests, distortion of facts and decisions in public pronouncements, and the elitism of specialists, technocrats, and bureaucrats, who short-circuit democratic decision making because of their presumed control of the necessary expertise.

Over the years, governments at all levels have developed control mechanisms for ensuring responsible decisions and actions by public managers and civil servants. Figure 6.1 organizes many of these sources of control. Some of the controls are formal, others informal. And some stem from internal sources, whereas others are provided by external sources. All of them are mechanisms for helping to avoid the pitfalls and barriers to administrative responsibility.

This exercise asks you to develop lists of specific examples of problem areas in administrative responsibility for three levels of govern-

*This introduction is largely derived from Grover Starling, *Managing the Public Sector* (Homewood, Ill.: The Dorsey Press, 1977), pp. 86–102. ©1977 by The Dorsey Press.

Internal	*External*
Executive orders, Policies, Procedures	Legislation Court interpretations
Professional codes Representative bureaucracy Public interest Moral philosophy of managers	Interest group representation Citizen participation Advisory groups Open hearings

FIGURE 6.1. Approaches for Ensuring Administrative Responsibility.

ment. And then it asks you to develop examples of specific control mechanisms which have been developed at each of those levels to deal with the problems you have identified. Discussion time will be used to examine some additional questions pertaining to difficulties in these areas.

B. Procedures

1. Form groups of from five to seven members. Assign to each group one of these three levels of government for discussion: city, state, federal. If possible, have at least one group for each level (*five minutes*).

2. Each group is to develop two lists from the perspective of its assigned level of government (*forty-five minutes*):
   a. Specific examples of problems with administrative responsibility (make sure you have enough detail for each problem that you can explain it to the full class).
   b. Specific examples of control mechanisms that have been developed to deal with the types of problems identified in (a).

3. Choose a spokesperson for the group and develop a presentation to the class explaining the problem areas and control mechanisms identified in step 2 (*ten minutes*).

4. Bring the groups back together for general discussion. Begin the discussion with each group presenting its lists of problem areas and control mechanisms. Then, proceed with the questions in the discussion section (*thirty minutes*).

C. Discussion and Conclusions

1. Are the problems different for different levels of government? Really? What are the similarities and differences?

2. Are the control mechanisms different at different levels of govern-
    ment? Really? What are the similarities and differences?

3. What can you do as a public manager to ensure your own (and your
    agency's) responsibility in decision making and actions? Would you
    actually do it? What conflicts arise?

4. Does it all seem easy? If so, why do so many examples of irresponsi-
    bility continue to get attention? Or, are the examples really the
    exceptions?

5. What did you miss? Were there any glaring oversights in the lists?
    Why or why not? What does this say about this group's attitudes
    and perceptions?

D. Assessment of Learning

Think about what you have done in this exercise. Try to identify two or
three major points that you have learned from this experience. What
meaning do these points have for you as an individual and for you as an
administrator? How might you put this learning to use outside the class?

Consider only what you have really learned. Don't try to figure
out what other participants say they learned, or what you think you
should have learned. If you feel you didn't learn anything, think about
why. What could you have done to get more out of the exercise? How
might the exercise have been structured differently to provide a better
learning experience? What could be done in later exercises to help make
them better learning experiences?

E. Selected Readings

1. Bailey, S.K., "Ethics and the public service," in R.C. Martin, ed., *Public Administration and Democracy* (Syracuse, N.Y.: Syracuse University Press, 1965), pp. 283–298.

2. Blau, P.M., *The Dynamics of Bureaucracy*, rev. ed. (Chicago: University of Chicago Press, 1963).

3. Downs, A., *Inside Bureaucracy* (Boston: Little, Brown, 1967).

4. Rourke, F.E., *Bureaucracy, Politics, and Public Policy* (Boston: Little, Brown, 1969).

5. Simmons, R.H., and Dvorin, E.P., *Public Administration* (Port Washington, N.Y.: Alfred Publishing Co., 1977).

6. Starling, G., *Managing the Public Sector* (Homewood, Il.: The Dorsey Press, 1977), ch. 4, "Administrative responsibility."

PART
II

Organization Behavior and Theory

PART II   Organization Behavior and Theory

Not only do public managers have to administer programs, budgets, and diverse constituencies, they must also work effectively with the people and the organizational systems within which these people operate. Indeed, many of the difficult problems of public administration arise from the "people" side of the job, rather than from the "technical" side. Part II presents a number of exercises which provide a look at and practice in some of the more prominent organizational and behavioral problems that must be dealt with and understood.

In the past, management books have stressed the "one best way" approach. That is, they have taught that there is one best way to structure an organization, one best way to manage a group, one best way to communicate with and motivate employees, etc. This one-best-way was often the style and structure that is identified as bureaucracy.

Bureaucracy may have been—and may still be—appropriate in certain settings. When the organizational environment—internally and externally—is relatively stable, reliance on rules and regulations and stabilized management systems is effective. But, as the exercises in this Part suggest, variety and lack of predictability are probably better descriptions of the environment of today's public organizations. Thus, these exercises stress flexibility and options instead of a one-best-way approach.

Exercise 7 provides an opportunity for looking at two options for ways to structure a service agency. Exercise 8 examines procedures for facilitating group effectiveness and change within work teams.

The next three exercises deal specifically with the superior-subordinate relationship. Exercise 9 provides practice in the managerial activity of performance appraisal of subordinates' work activities, with the chance to examine the likely results from different approaches to the performance appraisal interview. Exercise 10 looks at the outcomes from the use of different leadership styles. And exercise 11 takes a look at the emerging values of today's employees and how those values relate to management's options for motivating those employees.

The last exercise in this section, exercise 12, compares the results of various options for gathering the ideas and information necessary for writing the regulations to implement a new piece of legislation. Through this exercise, the student will gain a better understanding of some of the problems involving intra-agency communciation.

SECTION
A

Organizational Structure

EXERCISE 7

Organization of a CETA Agency: By Function or by Program?

Purpose

1. To understand the differences between organizing by function and organizing by program.
2. To assess the strengths and weaknesses of alternatives for organizing a CETA agency.

Preparation

None. For those not familiar with CETA, read appendix C.

Group Size

Fifteen (minimum), including exercise leader.

Time Requirement

A minimum of ninety minutes.

Physical Setting

A large room with movable tables and chairs or a couple of rooms in close proximity.

Related Issues

Staffing, delegation, coordination, staff development, job design.

A. Introduction

Division of work is the cornerstone of all modern organizations. Extensive and intensive division of work—that is, specialization—has made possible high levels of organizational productivity. Early administrative

73

theorists (Fayol 1949; Gulick and Urwick 1937; Taylor 1911) made it clear that effective organization demanded a high degree of specialization of tasks and a thorough division of labor. If each person concentrates on a particular segment of a larger task, he or she becomes a specialist; in this way employees can refine their knowledge and skills and become ever more proficient. Others are doing what they do best, all the tasks get done, and the larger goal is accomplished with ever increasing efficiency.

Division of work allows tasks to be divided to the point where large numbers of people have the capacity to learn the skills and knowledge required to perform the tasks. Thus, it greatly increases the availability of human resources. Because tasks done this way can be specified in detail, all persons doing the same task will do it in the same way. The service provided is relatively uniform and interchangeable. Obviously, with each person doing the same task the same way, people also become relatively interchangeable. These points enable management to more easily control the quality of performance and to find and correct deviations.

Nevertheless, recent research and experience indicates that, taken to extremes, too much specialization can result in a number of negative consequences. When tasks are minutely divided, work is not meaningful to the individual, with serious consequences for mental and physical health and willingness and ability to perform for the organization. Boring, monotonous jobs, lack of opportunity for development of personal skills, alienation from the employing organization, low self-esteem, withdrawal, and apathy are results often seen (*Work in America* 1973). The problems of supervision are greatly increased for the organization as it tries to coordinate the many specialists.

In short, specialization is a powerful tool for maximizing the effectiveness of organizations. It is such a common phenomenon that we normally don't pay much attention to it or its consequences. In this exercise, we will explore two alternative ways to organize an agency for providing services to CETA clients. One involves a high degree of specialization. And the other provides a less specialized (or more generalist) approach to division of work. The exercise will allow you to experience some of the implications of these two alternatives.

B. Procedure

The object for the two project staffs who are under contract to the local prime sponsor in this exercise is to prepare four clients to be job qualified. Both projects have staffs and budgets of similar sizes but are organized in different ways to pursue their objectives. Each project is to plan for and to contract with vendors to provide training, counseling, and health care services for the four clients. Read only the role description that defines the role to which you are assigned.

1. Organization (*five minutes*)
   a. The exercise leader will act as the prime sponsor contractor.
   b. Four persons will be chosen by the exercise leader to act as service vendors. These four persons will be designated as vendors A, B, C, and D.
   c. Two groups of five or more persons will be chosen to act as project staffs. One group shall be designated as project S (Get a Job). And the other will be designated as project G (Find a Job). Project S is organized with a high degree of specialization. Project G prefers to use a generalist staff. Each project group will involve the following roles:
      project director (one)
      clerical staff (one or more)
      professional staff (three or more)
   d. The director of project S is to assign professional staff in the following way:
      (1) One training specialist responsible for vendors A and B.
      (2) One counseling specialist responsible for vendor C.
      (3) One health care specialist responsible for vendor D.
   e. The director of project G is to assign professional staff so that each is responsible for all of the vendors.
2. Read the instructions for the role you have been designated to play (*fifteen minutes*).
3. Planning stage (*twenty minutes*)
   a. Each director is to hold a planning session with his or her staff, to discuss the following agenda:
      (1) Ensure that all staff members understand the exercise, their particular roles, and the objectives of their organization.
      (2) Review the clients' case histories.
      (3) Determine the types of services each client needs in order to become job qualified.
      (4) Delegate appropriate responsibilities to all staff members. Decide on a plan and budget for providing the necessary services to the clients (use form A).
   b. Vendors need to make sure that they are thoroughly familiar

with their roles during this phase, and have made all the preparations called for in the role descriptions.

4. Negotiation stage (*twenty minutes*)
   During this phase, the staff members of projects S and G will solicit client services from the appropriate vendors.
   a. Project directors supervise the implementation of their programs' plans.
   b. The professional staff are the only persons who negotiate and contract with the vendors in order to acquire services for their clients.
5. Debriefing and evaluation of exercise outcomes (*twenty minutes*)

C.   Discussion and Conclusions

1. Which form of organization accomplished its objectives? (Or, who came the closest?) Why?

2. What were the strengths (and weaknesses) of the two forms of organization? What problems were a result of the specialization or generalist nature of the staffs?

3. How was planning done? How long did it take? Who did it? Why?

4. What form of group leadership emerged? Why? Did it have anything to do with the way the group was organized? How directive or participative was it? Did the form of leadership change during the exercise? What impact did the leadership style have on the group?

5. What influence did the form of organization have on how the group did its negotiating and accomplished its tasks? Why?

D. Assessment of Learning

Think about what you have done in this exercise. Try to identify two or three major points that you have learned from this experience. What meaning do these points have for you as an individual and for you as an administrator? How might you put this learning to use outside the class?

Consider only what you have really learned. Don't try to figure out what other participants say they learned, or what you think you should have learned. If you feel you didn't learn anything, think about why. What could you have done to get more out of the exercise? How might the exercise have been structured differently to provide a better learning experience? What could be done in later exercises to help make them better learning experiences?

E. Selected Readings

Fayol, H., *General and Industrial Management*, C. Storrs, trans. (London: Sir Isaac Pitman and Sons, 1949).

Gulick, L., and Urwick, L., *Papers on the Science of Administration* (New York: Institute of Public Administration, 1937).

Litterer, J.A., *The Analysis of Organizations*, 2nd ed. (New York: John Wiley and Sons, 1973).

Melcher, A.J., *Structure and Process of Organizations* (Englewood Cliffs, N.J.: Prentice-Hall, 1976).

Taylor, F.W., *Scientific Management* (New York: Harper and Row, 1911).

Work in America, Report of a Special Task Force to the Secretary of HEW (Cambridge, Mass.:   MIT Press, 1973).

F.   Participant Roles

Client Histories

Client 1. Phil Cooper is a married, twenty-nine-year-old white man who was released from the state penitentiary five months ago after serving two years for armed robbery. During the last eight months he has searched constantly for a job but has been turned away from one employer after another because of his lack of a specific job skill. His working wife has remained married to him despite the hardships and has constantly endeavored to rebuild his self-esteem and courage, but lately Phil has turned to drinking. He had a severe argument with his wife this past weekend during which she threatened to leave him if he did not seek professional help for his problems of drinking and joblessness. Phil has worked a variety of unskilled jobs but he did complete a twelve-month course in radio electronics while serving in the U.S. Army before receiving a dishonorable discharge for belligerent action. Phil's wife works at a department store. Phil believes that his unemployment is incurable.

Client 2. Marian Russell, an eighteen-year-old black woman, is seeking training in order to find a job to support her family, which includes her mother and four younger sisters still in grade school. Her father, who had been working as a laborer, died six months ago of cancer. Marian had some training in business machines while attending high school from which she graduated last year. She would like to become a computer programmer but is not sure she has the ability. She is also worried about her physical health. She suffers from diabetes, and fears this may prevent her from performing well in a training program or a job situation. She lives in the ghetto.

Client 3. Juan Lopez, a twenty-five-year-old Hispanic, is married and has two children. He has been unemployed for nine months since being laid off from the local car bumper plant. He had been employed there for three years as an unskilled laborer on the assembly line. Juan has been addicted to heroin since he was nineteen. He has one arrest, but no conviction. Juan says he still uses drugs once in a while when he feels extremely pressured as he is now, but that the real problem he faces is reeducating himself to be an auto mechanic so he can find a good job to support his family.

Client 4. Janet Jacobs is a thirty-two-year-old white woman married to a man who lost both legs as a result of a car accident that was his fault. The accident occurred over a year ago, and they have been living on their savings, which are nearly depleted. Janet had worked as a keypunch operator for a few years before they were married ten years ago, but has been busy raising their two school-aged children since then. She is in great need of obtaining a job in order to support her family. She is also having severe marital problems as a result of her husband's extreme dependency on her and his unrealistic attitude against her seeking employment.

Role Descriptions

Project Director of Project S, Get A Job. You are the project director of project S. You have contracted CETA funds from the county prime sponsor to provide job training for four "paper people" described in the preceding case histories. You have three staff members who are specialists in negotiating particular types of client services. The first is a training specialist, the second is a counseling specialist, and the third is a health care specialist. Each staff member is an expert on the vendors that provide client services related to his or her specialty. You also have one clerk whose responsibilities are outlined in the clerical instructions. You should familiarize yourself with these administrative procedures before calling your staff meeting.

This is the contract you have negotiated with the prime sponsor:

Program Get a Job is granted $4,000 to provide four people with the training, counseling, and health care necessary in order for each of the four clients to be job qualified by the end of phase two of this exercise. If each of the four people are evaluated as job qualified by the prime sponsor during phase three of the exercise, the contract will be renewed. If not, the contract will be cancelled and you and your staff will become unemployment statistics.

Job Qualified Criteria:

1. Client must receive training certificate from vendor.
2. Client must receive a job finding techniques appointment with vendor C.

Specialist Staff Members of Project S. You are responsible for familiarizing yourself with the vendor services and requirements appropriate to your staff specialty. Do not read information on other vendors. You will be called upon in a planning meeting to supply your specialist's knowledge for planning and budgeting purposes.

Clerical Staff Members of Project S. You are responsible for keeping each client's file up to date. You are also responsible for check writing and bookkeeping. This will include the following tasks:

1. Writing checks for client services and keeping cost records per service per client. You may use form A for keeping records. Blank checks are printed on form C. Do not disburse checks to your staff for client services without first obtaining your director's signature on them.
2. Obtaining and filing job finding techniques appointment slips for each client.
3. Obtaining and filing training certificates for each client.
4. Giving prime sponsor results of program during evaluation phase.

Project Director of Project G, Find A Job. You are the project director of project G. You have contracted CETA funds from the county prime sponsor to provide job training for the four "paper people" described in the preceding client histories. You have three staff members who are generalists in negotiating client services. Each has been cross trained to negotiate training, counseling, and health care services with the corresponding service vendor for the clients. You also have one clerical staff whose responsibilities are described elsewhere on this page. You should familiarize yourself with these clerical procedures before calling your staff meeting.

This is the contract you have negotiated with the prime sponsor:

Program Find a Job is granted $4,000 to provide four people with the training counseling, and health care necessary in order for each of the four clients to be job qualified by the end of phase two of this exercise. If each of the four people are evaluated as job qualified by the prime sponsor during phase three of the exercise, the contract will be renewed. If not, the contract will be cancelled and you and your staff will become unemployment statistics.

Criteria for being job qualified:

1. Client must receive training certificate from vendor.
2. Client must receive a job finding techniques appointment with vendor D.

Generalist Staff Members of Project G. You are responsible for familiarizing yourself with all vendor services (training, counseling, and health care). You will be called on in a staff meeting to supply your generalist's knowledge for planning and budgeting purposes.

Clerical Staff Member of Project G. You are responsible for keeping each client's file up to date. You are also responsible for check writing and bookkeeping. This will include the following tasks:

1. Writing checks for client services and keeping cost records per service per client. You may use form A for keeping records. Blank checks are printed on form C. Do not disburse checks to your staff for client services without first obtaining your director's signature on them.
2. Obtaining and filing job finding techniques appointment slips for each client.
3. Obtaining and filing training certificates for each client.
4. Giving prime sponsor results of program during evaluation phase.

Vendors* (and Required Reading for Generalist and Specialist Staff Members of Projects S and G).

Training

Vendor A

Your training center is organized to provide vocational education. Your organization requires each client to receive a medical examination before acceptance. Your organization offers the following training certificates upon the completion of the required designated courses:

*Vendors only: Be sure to read your Special Instructions.

80

Certificate	Cost
1. Computer language certificate	
Required courses: introduction to computers	$150
computer languages	$750
2. Secretarial skills certificate	
Required courses: typing and filing	$500
ten key and full board adding machines	$250
3. Key punch certificate	
Required courses: introduction to computers	$150
key punch	$600
4. Office machine repair certificate	
Required course: office machine repair	$750

TRAINING CERTIFICATES: See Form D

Vendor B

Your training center is organized to provide vocational education. Your organization requires each client to receive a medical examination before acceptance. Your organization offers the following training certificates upon completion of the required designated subjects:

Certificate	Cost
1. Draftsman certificate	
Required courses: mechanical drawing	$350
blueprint reading	$350
2. Car body repair certificate	
Required course: car body repair	$750
3. Auto mechanic certificate	
Required courses: auto mech I	$250
auto mech II	$250
auto mech III	$250

TRAINING CERTIFICATES: See Form D

Counseling

Vendor C

Your counseling center is organized to provide the following types of services (each costs $100 per client):

1. alcoholism counseling
2. hard drug use counseling
3. marital and family counseling
4. ex-con community readjustment counseling
5. job skill aptitude evaluation
6. job finding techniques
7. job reorientation counseling
8. day care center

81

Note to Counseling Vendor C: You will have to supply clients with appointment slips for five through eight. Client must have training certificate before appointment can be made. See form E for counseling service appointment slips.

Health Care

Vendor D
Your health care center is organized to provide the following services:

1. dental	$250 per month
2. general medical	$ 50 per visit
3. psychiatric	$100 per client
4. methadone treatment for hard drug addicts	$250 per client
5. alcohol detox treatment	$250 per client

HEALTH CARE RECEIPTS: See Form F

Special Instructions for Vendors Only

Vendor A: You have no room left in your computer programming course.
Vendor B: You have only three spaces left in your auto mechanic certificate program.
Vendor C: Anyone asking for a skill aptitude evaluation for a client should be told the following: your client has a high skill aptitude for repairing office machines.
Vendor D: All medical requests other than dental and medical examinations are to be diagnosed as psychosomatic and an appointment must be made with the psychiatrist before you can approve the person for vendor training.

General Note to Vendors: Each program agency is attempting to service the same four clients. To avoid confusion, label all clients' paper work with a 1 or 2 in front of the name: 1 for those clients being serviced by Program Get A Job, and 2 for those clients being serviced by Program Find A Job. Be sure to collect checks for all the services that you provide for the clients.

Instructions for Exercise Leader
After the negotiation stage is completed, the exercise leader (prime sponsor) should collect the client qualifying materials from projects S and G and from the vendors. Based on the criteria for job qualification (each client must have a training certificate plus an appointment for counseling on job finding techniques), determine the degree of success of each program. Success for each program is determined by the number of clients who are job qualified within the allotted budget ($4,000). Be prepared to provide this information during the discussion.

Thus, each job-qualified client from each program will have the following:

1. medical examination receipt
2. training certificate
3. appointment slip for job finding techniques counseling

And total expenditures for each program should not exceed $4,000.

PHASE 1   FORM A
PLANNING AND BUDGETING

Client	*Type of Training/Cost*	*Type of Counseling/Cost*	*Type of Health Care/Cost*
1			
2			
3			
4			

Total Training Cost:
Counseling Cost:
Health Care Cost:

_____

Projected Program Cost:

	Program S	Program G
Total clients job qualified		
Training costs		
Counseling costs		
Health care costs		
Total costs		

FORM C
CHECKS FOR PROJECT CLERK

To _____ **From** _____ **$** _____ **Project Director Sign.** _____ **Client's Name** _____	

FORM D
TRAINING CERTIFICATES

To _____ From. _____ $ _____ Project Director Sign. _____ Client's Name _____	

FORM E
COUNSELING SERVICES: APPOINTMENT SLIPS

Appointment

To Program _____

From Vendor C $ _____

For Client _____

Service Appointment _____

FORM F
HEALTH CARE RECEIPTS

Receipt To Program _____ From Vendor D $ _____ For Client _____ Service Provided _____	

SECTION
B

Organization Design and Team Building

EXERCISE 8

Work Group Effectiveness and Organizational Change

Purpose

1. To develop recognition of the dimensions of work group effectiveness.
2. To develop the ability to observe group processes.
3. To understand methods of inhibiting and facilitating work group effectiveness.
4. To identify how team-building techniques might be used to increase group effectiveness.

Preparation

Read sections A and F prior to coming to class.

Group Size

Any size (minimum of six participants).

Time Requirement

Two hours thirty-five minutes. This exercise might best be used during two classroom periods, with steps 1 to 6 done during the first meeting and step 7 and the discussion finished during the second session.

Physical Setting

Movable chairs or facilities for small groups to meet without disturbing other groups.

This exercise is adapted from Donald F. Harvey, Donald R. Brown, *An Experiential Approach to Organization Development*, ©1976, pp. 57, 59, 60, 61, 62, 63, 64. Reprinted by permission of Prentice-Hall, Inc., Englewood Cliffs, New Jersey.

Related Issues

Communication, information sharing, leadership, group roles, collaboration versus competition, group problem solving, intergroup conflict, intragroup conflict, organizational politics, organizational change.

A.   Introduction

Much work in public organizations is done in groups. How effectively the work gets done, therefore, is often influenced by how well a group functions. The degree of effective communication and information sharing, shared acceptance of responsibilities within the group, knowledge and use of good feedback procedures and nondefensive interpersonal relations, and the amount of ability to diagnose the group and any of its problems all help determine the effectiveness of any work group.

During the last thirty years, a number of techniques have been developed to aid work teams and organizations in improving their work process. The assumptions underlying these techniques suggest that improved group processes will result in improved productivity and group effectiveness. Basic to these techniques is a sequential process of actions that effective groups seem to follow. These steps are displayed in figure 8.1.

As figure 8.1 shows, once someone in an organization says, "We have a problem," there is a need to do some thorough data gathering to identify more carefully the real sources of the problem. This awareness that there is a problem might be based on intuition or on any number of indicators such as high turnover, too many complaints and grievances, absenteeism, or poor quality or quantity of work. All work group members should be involved even at the data gathering stage. They can design and carry out the data gathering. And, surely, they should be involved in the organization and interpretation of the data. Then they can help determine what to do about the problems identified by these data.

Data can be gathered through written records and materials, formal but unobtrusive observation, interviewing of personnel in the organization, survey instruments of different kinds, and so forth. Consultants can help with the data gathering stages, particularly if they don't try to do it all themselves.

The choice of interventions and the implementation and monitoring of changes should also be a highly participative process. Many groups have had little practice at this type of participation, though. It makes

92

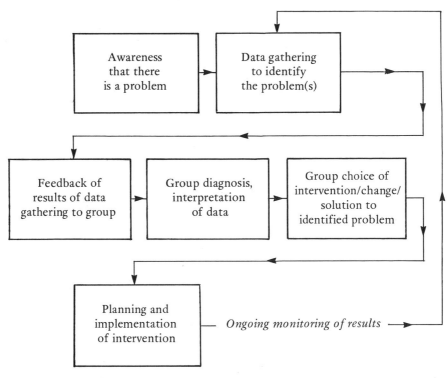

FIGURE 8.1   The Change Process in an Effective Group or Organization

sense to go slow and learn the skills of participation, idea generation, and idea implementation in stages. Consultants can often help an organization through these learning stages.

The last step in this process is the ongoing collection of data about the results of implemented changes as well as about new or other problems. Effective groups seem to have well-developed skills for regularly assessing and diagnosing themselves and prescribing and implementing the changes necessary for them to regain or retain effectiveness.

Obviously, these procedures themselves help a group to learn to be more effective, or, at least, to identify and assess problem areas. The solution to these problems may involve anything from better goal setting and goal communication to improved decision-making skills and other technical abilities, from better interpersonal skills to improved budgeting and control abilities. Most of the other exercises in this book are designed to improve such skills. This exercise is designed to improve the skills involved with group change and identification and assessment of organizational problem areas.

B. Procedure

1. Prior to class, read sections A and F.

2. Form groups of six members with each member taking the role of one of the five service directors or the administrator. If there is not an even number of participants in multiples of six, assign the odd persons to a group or groups to assist one or more of the service directors in their roles. Each participant should then read only his or her assigned role (see section F). In the group meeting, each participant has the concern of protecting his/her service area by trying to gain additional funding *as well as* benefiting the overall community and SACOG (*fifteen minutes*).

3. Before the group meets, each participant should complete the team effectiveness profile (individual form), found at the end of this exercise, with his/her prediction of how well the group will perform in this problem-solving situation (*ten minutes*).

4. The administrator of SACOG has called a meeting of the five area directors. He or she will explain the task to be performed (*thirty-five minutes*).

5. Return to the team effectiveness profile (individual form) and, acting alone, fill in your perception of how your group actually performed. Use an X this time to record your response (*ten minutes*).

6. As a group, compute and record group averages and low and high scores for predictions and actual performance on the team effectiveness profile (group form)(*ten minutes*).

7. As a group, analyze the data from the team effectiveness forms. What problems can be identified through these data? What areas are shown by these data to be areas of concern for group productivity? After identifying two or three specific problem areas, generate the following set of solution ideas for those problems (*forty-five minutes*):

   a. The end result that would be desired in each problem area.

   b. The organizational changes, interventions, training, etc., that would achieve those end results.

   c. An action plan for the implementation of each suggested organizational change, with specific actions to be taken, by whom, within what time frame, with which results to be reviewed and evaluated at what point in time by whom.

8. Discussion (*thirty minutes*).

C.   Discussion and Conclusions

1. How did the group analyze the data generated by the team effectiveness forms? Does there appear to be more and less effective methods for analysis of this type of data? What methods seem to provide awareness and knowledge which can be acted on?

2. Did the group jump to conclusions too quickly? Did the group move too quickly to development of solutions, without fully looking at the nature of the problem(s)? What difference does that make?

3. Did the group members express the same behaviors in the analysis of the data as they did in the decision-making situation itself? Why or why not? What does this indicate about group processes? What can be done to change this situation?

4. What skills for effective group performance seem to be missing? How might the group develop these skills? Where might you (or individual members) get the information about how to develop these skills?

D. Assessment of Learning

Think about what you have done in this exercise. Try to identify two or three major points that you have learned from this experience. What meaning do these points have for you as an individual and for you as an administrator? How might you put this learning to use outside the class?

Consider only what you have really learned. Don't try to figure out what other participants say they learned, or what you think you should have learned. If you feel you didn't learn anything, think about why. What could you have done to get more out of the exercise? How might the exercise have been structured differently to provide a better learning experience? What could be done in later exercises to help make them better learning experiences?

E. Selected Readings

Francis, D., and Woodcock, M., *People at Work: A Practical Guide to Organizational Change* (La Jolla, Calif.: University Associates, 1975).

French, W.L., and Bell, C.H., Jr., *Organization Development*, 2d ed. (Englewood Cliffs, N.J.: Prentice-Hall, 1978).

Huse, E., *Organization Development and Change* (St. Paul, Minn.: West Publishing Co., 1975).

Margulies, N., and Rais, A.P., *Conceptual Foundations of Organizational Development* (New York: McGraw-Hill, 1978).

Margulies, N., and Wallace, J., *Organizational Change: Techniques and Applications* (Glenview, Ill.: Scott, Foresman and Co., 1973).

Napier, R.W., and Gershenfeld, M.K., *Groups: Theory and Experience* (Boston: Houghton Mifflin, 1973).

Schein, E., *Process Consultation: Its Role in Organization Development* (Reading, Mass.: Addison-Wesley, 1969).

F. Working Documents

SACOG Background Information

SACOG, Southern Area Council of Governments, is a regional organization of several large counties and their towns in a sparsely populated area of a western state. SACOG administers a variety of social services, including those relating to (1) drug abuse, (2) alcohol rehabilitation, (3) marriage counseling, (4) mental health, and (5) employment training. These five social service areas are organized to be separate from each other in terms of personnel and financing. They are administered from a central office located in the largest town in the region. Each of the five social services has its own offices located throughout the region.

SACOG receives financing from area, state, and federal governments and private grants. The total amount for this year is $10 million. The funds received have been increasing by an annual rate of 15 percent for the past five years.

Several days ago SACOG received an invitation to apply for a special $500,000 grant from a private foundation. The wording of the invitation indicated that the application would have to be very specific, which means that only one of the five areas would be able to apply for and receive the grant. Because of the large number of minority groups in the area and because SACOG is one of the most advanced and progressive social programs in the West, there is a high probability of SACOG receiving the grant.

The administrator of SACOG decided to call a meeting of the five social service directors for the purpose of deciding which one of their areas will be selected to apply for the grant. The director did some homework and came up with six criteria he believes to be relevant in the selection: (1) the past successes and failures, (2) the number of minorities served, (3) the number of people receiving services, (4) the availability of facilities in the region, (5) the anticipated results, and (6) the needs of the community.

Role Descriptions

SACOG Administrator. As SACOG administrator you are responsible for coordinating the five programs. These programs are fairly well isolated in their operation, and it is up to you to ensure coordination.

The five directors are not only competent in their own program areas but are all good administrators. Each knows his field and firmly believes that his program can definitely benefit the community.

Though you do have final decision-making authority, you would like to ensure continued commitment to SACOG by allowing the five directors to help you select the service area that should be permitted to apply for the $500,000 grant. Avoid taking a position until you have heard from all directors because you are reluctant to influence the decision unduly. You would prefer not to use voting to make a decision but instead reach a consensus. It is necessary that a decision be reached by the end of the meeting.

In the SACOG background information, it is mentioned that you have called a meeting of the five directors. At the beginning of the meeting you will need to explain what is to be decided, the directors' roles and your own role in the meeting, and the procedure the meeting will take.

Mental Health Director. As director of mental health it is your responsibility to administer the outpatient facilities. The mental health program hires trained and experienced psychologists. The services are entirely on an outpatient basis. In fact, the area has no mental health facilities except the outpatient services provided by SACOG, so the community definitely needs the services. Records indicate you have worked with seven hundred people in the past year.

The facilities are located in the three large towns in the area. If people needing services live in outlying areas, they must travel to one of the towns. Because of the large geographical area to be covered and the salaries of the staff, it has not been practical to provide mobile services.

The department has been successful in its work and is one of the better out-patient clinics in the country. Originally there was some reluctance to use the facilities, but time and success seem to have changed this. Future programs will probably be just as successful. Various pilot programs have been tested in conjunction with a state university, and several have received wide attention. More extensive use of these new programs is planned.

There seem to be very few minority people seeking SACOG services. This can partly be attributed to a long history of misunderstanding of the services offered. Furthermore, a study, though not conclusive, shows that there are few mental problems among the minority population. There seems to be a strong indication that many of the people using the services have been referred to you as a last resort.

Although your program is not perfect, you believe it and the community could greatly benefit from the use of the grant.

Marriage and Family Counseling Director. As director of marriage and family counseling it is your responsibility to administer counseling programs in such areas as child abuse, husband-wife relationships, and runaway children. The statistics show past success for those cases in which your program has been involved. Follow-up studies are favorable. In the case of husband-wife counseling, the divorce rate is lower than the average. In most of the child abuse cases, children are kept in the natural home instead of in foster homes. Runaway children who have been located and brought back home usually do not run away again, and this has been attributed to family counseling.

There are centers in the three large towns, and several mobile trailers are used to serve the rural communities. The number receiving services has been increasing, up to 3,500 cases annually, although the facilities are geared to more. There seems to be a feeling among staff workers that people are hesitant to confide problems they may have with their marriage or children. Minorities use the services, although no more or no less than their numbers in the census figures would indicate.

Based on past data, there is a fairly high rate of success once a family comes in for help, but not all families needing help come in. The continued police reports of child abuse show a definite need for the services. The divorce rate is still high, though there are signs it may be dropping. You would like to start working with families before their problems reach the stage of a runaway child or divorce, but you have not been successful in identifying these families and getting them to accept help. Despite this obstacle, it seems that with your past success rate and the community's continuing need for services, the future looks promising.

Although your area is not perfect, you believe it and the community could greatly benefit from the use of the grant.

Employment Training and Education Director. As director of training and education it is your responsibility to assist the so-called unemployable and those seeking new skills in obtaining skills needed for employment. Your department does not actually train people, but it arranges training and usually assists in the financing. Although the State Employment Commission and the Veterans Administration have similar services, there seem to be enough people unemployed and needing the services that all help is welcomed. Yours and the other agencies often work together and coordinate programs.

As virtually all people for whom training has been arranged have been able to obtain employment, you feel your area has been successful even though there is still a fairly high unemployment rate, particularly among minorities. For those minorities that you have been able to reach, there has been a respectable, though not overwhelming, acceptance and use of the services. But as your facilities are in the three large towns, the large minority group living in the rural area has received virtually no assistance. Furthermore, the statistics seem to indicate that even if you could arrange training for the minority group it might be difficult to find employment for them since jobs are not available.

The other day you were looking at some statistics that showed that 1,400 people had used the services of your area within the past year. Even though this was only 9 percent of the unemployed, it does seem to be a healthy indication that those needing the services are receiving them. Considering the increasing unemployment rate and your past success in training people, the future looks promising.

Although your program is not perfect, you believe it and the community could greatly benefit from the use of the grant.

Drug Abuse Director. As director of drug abuse it is your responsibility to administer the various programs to reduce drug abuse. These programs include educational efforts in the schools, churches, and other parts of the community, as well as for persons who may come in contact with a drug abuser—parents, teachers, police-officers, etc. In educational efforts alone you estimate that your staff has talked to about ten thousand people in the past year. Other programs are specifically directed to the drug abuser, and these programs include one-to-one and group counseling and a twenty-four-hour hot-line service. Records indicate that you have worked with nine hundred people in these specific programs, and there is no information available on the hot-line service.

Research conducted by a private agency indicates that the harsher drugs are readily available, particularly in the larger towns. Also, marijuana use is increasing in the school systems.

The facilities are concentrated in the three largest towns in the area. There is a toll-free number that is staffed twenty-four hours a day. Efforts are being made to serve the smaller towns and rural areas, but it is costly and there are low returns. As a result you have decided to concentrate your efforts in the three large towns with well-equipped facilities. This strategy has caused some problems with serving minorities as there is a large minority population living in the rural areas.

Despite some problems in gaining acceptance from the larger segments of the community, your program is making substantial progress. Although drug abuse is increasing, studies indicate that the situation could have been worse if your staff had not been active. Follow-up studies on people who have been counseled by your staff indicate a favorable success rate. Considering the increasing availability of drugs and your program's past success, the future looks promising.

Although your program is not perfect, you believe it and the community could greatly benefit from the use of the grant.

Alcohol Education and Rehabilitation Director. As director of alcohol rehabilitation it is your responsibility to administer and coordinate various programs. These programs include educational efforts directed at schoolchildren and other potential users as well as people who may interface with potential abusers, such as teachers, employers, and ministers. You estimate that your staff has talked to about 10,000 people in the past year. Another phase of the program includes working directly with alcoholics on an individual and on a group basis, and records show that about 1,100 people have used these services in the past year.

A recent independent study shows that alcoholism exists in all sections of the community and involves a variety of ages, occupations, economic levels, and ethnic backgrounds. As the community is being increasingly educated regarding the dangers of alcoholism, there is more of a willingness to recognize the problem and to solve it.

The past success has been outstanding. Various experimental rehabilitation techniques have been tried, and several have been successful and have received wide publicity. The more traditional programs have also been used extensively. Even though you have a well-trained staff, you rely to a great extent on volunteer workers.

The services are offered throughout the area. As much as possible you rely on facilities furnished by churches, individuals, and communities. The use of volunteer workers and available facilities has permitted service to the isolated rural communities where a large minority population lives. The number of minority members taking advantage of the facilities has been increasing, perhaps because minority members are now employed as part of the staff and as volunteers.

Although your program is not perfect, you believe it and the community could greatly benefit from the use of the grant.

TEAM EFFECTIVENESS PROFILE
INDIVIDUAL FORM

INSTRUCTIONS: For each question, fill in your prediction of how your group will perform by circling the appropriate number.

1. Degree of cooperation:

   Low _____ High
   1   2   3   4   5   6   7

2. Degree of team member motivation:

   Low _____ High
   1   2   3   4   5   6   7

3. Degree of member satisfaction with this group activity:

   Low _____ High
   1   2   3   4   5   6   7

4. Amount of information sharing during this group situation:

   Low _____ High
   1   2   3   4   5   6   7

5. Degree of decision making through full discussion, acceptance, and consensus:

   Low _____ High
   1   2   3   4   5   6   7

6. Degree of conflict or competition during group decision making:

   Low _____ High
   1   2   3   4   5   6   7

7. Degree of quality of the group's decision:

   Low _____ High
   1   2   3   4   5   6   7

8. Degree of speed with which decisions are made:

   Low _____ High
   1   2   3   4   5   6   7

9. Degree of overall participation and acceptance of responsibility for getting a good final decision:

   Low _____ High
   1   2   3   4   5   6   7

TEAM EFFECTIVENESS PROFILE
GROUP FORM

INSTRUCTIONS: For each *question, fill in your prediction of how your grou group will perform by circling the appropriate number.*

1. Degree of cooperation:

   Low _____ *High*

   1   2   3   4   5   6   7

2. Degree of team member motivation:

   Low _____ *High*

   1   2   3   4   5   6   7

3. Degree of member satisfaction with this group activity:

   Low _____ *High*

   1   2   3   4   5   6   7

4. Amount of information sharing during this group situation:

   Low _____ *High*

   1   2   3   4   5   6   7

5. Degree of decision making through full discussion, acceptance, and consensus:

   Low _____ *High*

   1   2   3   4   5   6   7

6. Degree of conflict or competition during group decision making:

   Low _____ *High*

   1   2   3   4   5   6   7

7. Degree of quality of the group's decision:

   Low _____ *High*

   1   2   3   4   5   6   7

8. Degree of speed with which decisions are made:

   Low _____ *High*

   1   2   3   4   5   6   7

9. Degree of overall participation and acceptance of responsibility for getting a good final decision:

   Low _____ *High*

   1   2   3   4   5   6   7

SECTION
C

Human Behavior in Organizations

EXERCISE 9

Developing Effective Administrators: The Performance Appraisal

Purpose

1. To practice skills in performance appraisal and supervision of subordinates.
2. To develop skills in communication and problem solving.

Preparation

Read the introduction.

Group Size

Any size.

Time Requirement

Fifty to seventy minutes.

Physical Setting

Movable chairs or facilities for small groups to meet without disturbing other groups.

Related Issues

Leadership, group decision making and problem solving, power, interpersonal communication, organizational communication, and life, work, and career roles.

This exercise was developed by Dennis R. Briscoe from one by D.D. Bowen in *Experiences in Management and Organizational Behavior* by D.T. Hall, D.D. Bowen, R.J. Lewicki, and F.S. Hall. Copyright ©1975, John Wiley & Sons, Inc. Reprinted by permission of John Wiley & Sons, Inc.

A. Introduction

Any kind of system, whether it be a person, organization, or spacecraft, needs feedback from its environment to tell how close it is to being on target in achieving its objectives. One of the most important and useful sources of feedback to an employee is his or her supervisor. However, in the day-to-day course of our work experiences, we usually obtain little direct feedback on our performance from our supervisors—and we give an equal amount to our own subordinates.

One of the most common mechanisms for feedback between supervisors and subordinates is the performance appraisal discussion. In many organizations this is a formal process in which the supervisor fills out a standard form describing the employee's work and the employee, after discussing it with the supervisor, signs it. It is then sent to higher-level managers and is finally placed in the employee's personnel file.

Senior managers in most organizations will describe their performance appraisal systems in detail, stressing the requirements, such as the employee's signature, which ensure that the appraisal will, in fact, be conducted. However, when employees are asked about their performance appraisals, the response is often a blank stare. Many employees do not even know what a performance appraisal is. Others report that it is conducted in a cursory manner; many seem to be conducted in brief encounters in the hallway or by the coffee pot. Thus, there is a mysterious process whereby the performance appraisal is there when we talk to senior managers, but it's gone when we talk to employees. For this reason, the process has been dubbed the "vanishing performance appraisal" (Hall and Lawler 1969).

One of the reasons that performance appraisals disappear is that supervisors feel uncomfortable giving feedback in a one-to-one encounter. One reason they feel uncomfortable about it is that they have never developed the necessary skills. The purpose of this exercise is for you to begin to develop performance appraisal skills.

First, let us consider two different approaches to performance appraisal. Let us say you agree with Douglas McGregor (1967) on the following seven propositions:

Human Growth Potential
1. People are capable of growing in a social climate that permits and encourages growth.
2. People tend to grow when they can achieve their own goals by achieving those of the organization.

The Role of Communication and Feedback

3. Feedback is necessary for the survival and growth of any system.
4. Effective problem solving requires open exchange of information.
5. Transactional management (where power is shared) facilitates communication.

Effective Versus Ineffective Communication

6. People tend to become defensive when threatened; that is, hostile, protective behavior, overt compliance, and selective or distorted perception result.
7. People will use information if they find it helpful in achieving their goals.

What then, are the implications of these propositions for performance appraisal and the supervision of subordinates?

One important implication is that a problem-solving approach to performance appraisal is probably going to get more results than the tell-and-sell method. These two approaches are identified by Maier (1958), who describes the objectives, assumptions, employee reactions, and supervisor skills associated with each method.

The tell-and-sell method, which is the more commonly applied of the two, has two objectives: (1) to communicate evaluation and (2) to persuade the employee to improve. It is based upon four assumptions: (1) the employee desires to correct weaknesses if he or she knows them, (2) any person can improve if she or he so chooses, (3) a superior is qualified to evaluate a subordinate, and (4) people profit from criticism and appreciate help.

The skills required on the part of the supervisor are salesmanship and patience. The employee usually reacts in three ways: (1) suppressed defensive behavior, (2) attempts to cover hostility, and (3) a little change in performance.

The objective of the problem-solving method is to stimulate growth and development in the employee. It is based upon three assumptions: (1) growth can occur without correcting faults, (2) discussing job problems leads to improved performance, and (3) discussion develops new ideas and mutual interests.

The skills required of the supervisor are: (1) listening and reflecting feelings, (2) reflecting ideas, (3) using exploratory questions, and (4) summarizing. The reaction is often problem-solving behavior and employee commitment to the changes or objectives discussed (because they are his or her ideas).

107

B. Procedure

1. Small groups of from four to six ai   ormed by the group leader. Half of each group is assigned to i(:ify with the role of Chris Marshall and the other half with the   e of Dave Jones. Read *only* the role description you have been as   ed. Then one Chris and one Dave will role play the described p   )rmance appraisal, with the other group members observing t   procedures and behaviors demonstrated (*five minutes*).

2. The role playing takes place in as :   y rounds as it takes for all members of each group to perform ɛ   e. First, one pair (one Chris .and one Dave) act out their roles for   )ut five minutes, or until an impasse is reached. Then a second ɍ   and then the third pair play the roles (*about twenty minutes*).

3. During this step, members of the grɩ   should provide feedback to the persons who played the roles oᴉ   ᴉve Jones about the perfor mance appraisal technique(s) they ᴉ   :ed. Observers should be as specific and descriptive as they can.

4. Discussion (*fifteen minutes*).

C. Discussion and Conclusions

1. What did Chris and Dave do to faci   e the discussion? to hinder the discussion?

2. What evidence did you see of th   ll-and-sell method? of the problem-solving method?

3. How was Chris reacting to the methɩ   that Dave used?

108

4. What could Dave or Chris have done differently to help the discussion?

5. Which method of performance appraisal is most likely to occur? Why?

6. What steps can the supervisor take to encourage a problem-solving discussion?

D. Assessment of Learning

Think about what you have done in this exercise. Try to identify two or three major points that you have learned from this experience. What meaning do these points have for you as an individual and for you as an administrator? How might you put this learning to use outside the class?

Consider only what you have really learned. Don't try to figure out what other participants say they learned, or what you think you should have learned. If you feel you didn't learn anything, think about why. What could you have done to get more out of the exercise? How might the exercise have been structured differently to provide a better learning experience? What could be done in later exercises to help make them better learning experiences?

E. Selecte   'eadings

Hall, D.T., and Lawler, E.E., III, "Unused potential in research and development organizations," *Research Management*, 12 (1969): 339-354.

ellogg, M.S., *What to Do about Performance Appraisal*, rev. ed. (New York: American Management Associations, 1975).

inson, H., "Management by whose objectives?" *Harvard Business Review*, July/ gust 1970, 125-134.

M egor, D., *The Professional Manager* (New York: McGraw-Hill, 1967)

Mc   gor, D., "An uneasy look at performance appraisal," *Harvard Business Review*, M   June 1967, 89-94.

Maie '.R.F., *The Appraisal Interview* (New York: Wiley, 1958).

Meye   H., Kay, E., and French, J.R.P., Jr., "Split roles in performance appraisal," Har *Business Review*, January/February 1967, 123-129.

Oberg,   "Make performance appraisal relevant," *Harvard Business Review*, Janua 'ebruary 1972, 61-67.

F. Participant Roles

Performance Appraisal Roles

Chris Marshall,   'artment Head, Title I

You have just i   \ notified that your boss, Dave Jones, the director of the Bigville City-County Em   vment and Training Consortium, wants to see you in his office. As you walk to I   'ffice, you wonder what Dave wants to see you about. It might be one of two thir.

Maybe Dave i.   ing to promote you to the vacant assistant director's position. Several times durin&   ¿ past year he has indicated that he was thinking along those lines. As Dave put it,   vou proved yourself as Title I supervisor, the job would be yours. Well, your recc   'ertainly indicates you deserve the promotion! Placements have never been highe   d you have guided the staff to an effective solution of every problem that has   ne up. You are *very proud* of your many accomplishments.

Or Dave might wan   respond to your memo of last week on recruitment of planners and project direct   You have recommended:

1. offering higher salaries in   \es of attracting better quality personnel
2. instituting a tighter person   screening procedure to weed out incompetent and irresponsible applicants

Although you are very pro   of your accomplishments in the Title I department, the one problem that bothers you is the quality of the professional staff in the department. You have lost several lately, but you were glad to see most of them go. Most of them were sullen, irresponsible, and not very bright. Most were already in jobs over their heads, and none had potential for advancement.

Trying to improve the performance of your subordinates has been a constant drain on your energies. No matter how much coaching, pleading, encouraging, and threatening you do, it seems as if you have to double-check all of their work to be sure it is done correctly. Through your watchfulness you have corrected mistakes that could have proven very embarrassing for the consortium.

Dave Jones is an old personal friend, and you have enjoyed working for him.

At this point, you enter Dave's office.

Dave Jones, Director of Bigville City-County Employment and Training Consortium
You have just asked Chris Marshall to come to your office for a conference. Marshall is the Title I supervisor for the consortium. In most respects, you regard Marshall as an ideal administrator. Chris is efficient, intelligent, and displays great initiative, creativity, and unquestionable integrity. Under Marshall's guidance, placements have steadily increased, and numerous potential problems have been averted. Moreover, Chris is a personal friend.

You have called Chris to your office to discuss a problem which has been bothering you for the last year or so. Despite Chris's many virtues, there is one major problem. Younger staff in the department refuse to work for Marshall. No Title I project director will stay with the consortium for more than six months. They complain that Chris is authoritarian and never allows them to handle problems or projects on their own. Marshall is constantly looking over their shoulders and telling them exactly how to conduct even the most trivial aspects of their jobs.

You would like to appoint Marshall to the vacant position of assistant director. At the same time, you are afraid you may have to terminate Marshall for the good of the consortium. You have spoken to Chris several times in the past about this problem, and you feel that you have made it clear that the promotion depends on Chris's having prepared a successor—someone to take over the Title I job when Chris is promoted.

Recently, so many bright young people have left the consortium, you are determined that Chris must reverse this trend or leave the consortium himself.

(You are a little behind in your paperwork and you are not aware of any memo Chris might have sent you recently. If Chris mentions a memo, say that you have not had a chance to read it yet.)

At this point, Chris enters your office in answer to your call.

111

EXERCISE 10

Leadership in a Decision Dilemma: Who Wins at Greater Area Community College?

Purpose

1. To examine and evaluate the effects of differing leadership styles on the behavior and performance of group decision makers.
2. To examine the impacts of participative decision making (democracy) on the satisfaction and performance of the decision makers.
3. To experience the emergence of incompatibilities in roles and objectives of members of an organization and the consequent role conflicts.
4. To evaluate participative decision making as a technique for obtaining actionable decisions to which organizational members are committed.

Preparation

Assign roles to participants in advance.

Follow-up

Allow not less than one hour to debrief. Purposes 1, 3, and 4 cannot be achieved without substantial classroom discussion of the exercise and its outcomes.

This exercise was written by Dr. Barbara Karmel, Director of the Center for Business-Government Studies and Associate Dean, Atkinson Graduate School of Administration, Willamette University.

Group Size

Minimum of fifteen persons. As explained in the introduction, the exercise can be conducted with only ten persons, but the small number rules out the possibility of achieving purpose 1, the demonstration and evaluation of the impact of differing leadership styles on decision-making processes.

Time Requirement

Two hours.

Physical Setting

Room large enough for groups of five persons to meet separately, or differer   ooms for each group of five.

Related Issues

Group   cesses, and power and authority.

A.   Introduction

This ex   se is written to evoke, through role playing, a host of problems ei   intered when middle managers are asked to participate in
making   anizational decisions and to demonstrate the effect of different leac   hip styles on their resolution. At Greater Area Community
College,   o new faculty positions have been authorized by the president, bι   he difficult decision of which particular departments will get
these ne   ositions has been delegated to those most immediately concerned,   dean and department supervisors. A meeting has been called
to resol   this question, that is, to make a participative decision.
Needless   say, we begin with a situation of scarce resources: there are
five hun   departments in need of additional staffing but only two
positions   his reality produces a zero-sum circumstance; what one
departmε   wins, another must lose.

To   npound the dilemma, persons participating in this decision
have diff   it needs, training, values, and responsibilities. You will note
that some of the persons (role players) are young and eager; others have
been worn down by years of fighting the bureaucracy. Some have substantial political clout and supervise programs that "earn the bread and
butter" for the college; others represent innovative programs that will

114

not pay off for years. The very mission of the college is at issue here. For these and other reasons, the exercise will evoke incompatible objectives between the departments and players

The result of these incompatible objectives will be role conflict, with attendant potential for ill-will and inappropriate decisions— affecting the meeting itself, future relationships among those involved, and the performance of the college in the future.

If a sufficient number of persons are participating in the exercise (fifteen or more), it is also possible to examine the effects of leadership style. Roles are supplied for three very different kinds of deans, serving very different functions in the meeting. To take a look at the impact of leadership style, compare the outcomes from groups led by deans 1, 2, and 3, based on both performance and satisfaction of the participants.

As in all role-playing exercises, it is crucially important for players to "get into the skin" of the persons whose roles they play. Take some time to think about who you are and what is important to you as you walk into the meeting. It is equally important to remember that, in the real world, tomorrow will come and you will still be working in and for the organization. During the exercise, avoid the temptation to ignore the future because "this is only a game."

Although this exercise uses a community college as the site of the decision dilemma, the phenomena it evokes are by no means limited to community colleges. The exercise is equally applicable to any organization in which the chief asks subordinates to make a participative decision. Whether you believe that the chief really intends to honor the subordinates' decision is, and should be, a matter of concern.

You are to assume a role as dean, department chairperson, or coordinator at Greater Area Community College, an innovative and highly regarded institution in the Pacific Northwest. You have recently been advised by the president that he has secured funding for two new faculty positions. The president has met with the Academic Council, the dean of instructional operations, and the associate deans to discuss departmental needs and has identified five departments which, for one reason or another, have highest priority for allocation of the two new positions. The question remains, however, as to which of the five departments shall be given the extra personnel. In accordance with the policy of the institution to encourage decision making at the lowest level, the dean of instructional operations has called a meeting of these five department representatives. The chairperson of the Mathematics Department, Lynn, has been at GACC for four years, has ten faculty members, and is forty-three years old. Believing that there is no real

115

TABLE 10.1   *Characteristics of Meeting Attendees*

Name		Years in Position	Number in Department	Age
Les	Dean of instructional operations	4		45
Jo	Electronics chairperson	8	11	47
Brett	Paradental/paramedical chairperson	1	7	28
Kelly	Language arts chairperson	5	19	42
Chris	Adult education coordinator	3	15	33

chance of being allocated either of the new positions, she may choose not to attend. Persons expected to attend the meeting are listed in table 10.1.

During the exercise, accept the facts as given in your role. Try to let your feelings develop in accordance with the role you have assumed. When events or questions arise which are not covered by the role, make up facts and take positions which are plausible and consistent with the spirit of your role.

Your task is to decide which one or two of the five departments are to receive the two new faculty positions.

B. Procedure

1. Prior to the period of time allowed for the exercise, the instructor should assign a role to each participant and give him or her the page number on which that role appears. The instructor must caution participants *not* to read the roles assigned to other persons or the follow-up comments. Random assignment of roles is suggested (*five minutes*).

    (Note: The role of Lynn, Math Department chairperson, can be assigned or omitted depending on the number of players. Each group must be composed of five players, six if Lynn's role is used.)

2. Allow a few minutes for each set of persons playing the same role (all Bretts, all Kellys, etc.) to meet and talk about the role they will play. This helps to make the role "take" (*ten minutes*).

3. In separate areas of the room, or separate rooms, each dean will call to order the meeting of five (or six) chairpersons and coordinators. The dean will announce that the meeting must be concluded in fifty

minutes and will then follow the instructions contained in the dean's role.

During the meeting, the instructor and other observers move among the groups making written notes on similarities and differences in performance of each group and satisfaction of its members. If the class cannot be broken down into groups of five or six, extra students should act as observers but should *not* intervene in the exercise.

4. At the end of fifty minutes, each group member should rate in writing (anonymously) the following five statements on a scale from 5 (high) to 1 (low) (*ten minutes*).

    My satisfaction with the exercise
    My satisfaction with the decisions
    My performance in the exercise
    My level of commitment to the decisions
    My evaluation of the dean's performance

    The dean or an observer averages these ratings for each group. Each group member then reads the roles of the other participants.

5. Discussion (*fifty minute minimum*).

C. **Discussion and Conclusions**
    1. Identify the dimensions on which the group roles were constructed— age, seniority, energy level, sense of mission and goal of GACC, rationale for needing additional staffing in each department, etc.

    2. Each group reports on the strengths and weaknesses of its performance and the feelings of its members.

    3. Compare and discuss the average ratings made in step 4, above. Focus on similarities and differences in these ratings and the reasons for them.

117

4. Evaluate different leadership styles and participative decision making as an organizational technique. Include both the good and the bad news. To assist in this task, it will be helpful for participants to take time to read the discussion questions. Follow-up comments (section F) should be read at the conclusion of the session, before participants leave.

Discussion Questions

1. How did your group stack up on the following checklist?
   a. *Outcome*: Decision made? (or abdicated?)
   Sense of involvement and commitment to organization?
   Perception of upward influence by group members?
   Decision criteria explicitly identified?
   (before the decision was made?)
   Probable impact of the decision?
   b. *Process*: Shared participation in the meeting?
   Active listening?
   Sufficient skill and knowledge to make the decision?
   Full and complete flow of information?
   Effective leadership by the dean?

2. How could your group have been more effective?

3. What part did personalities play in this process? (or was it the role taken by each person?)

4. How did the role of Dean Helpem (facilitator), Dean Leavitt (abdicator), or Dean Pushin (manipulator) influence the decision process?

5. Did your group pay attention to the issues of
   a. equity between members?
   b. clarity of purpose and objectives?
   c. specificity of outcomes?
   d. flexibility for the future (while avoiding promises that cannot be kept)?

D. Assessment of Learning

Think about what you have done in this exercise. Try to identify two or three major points that you have learned from this experience. What meaning do these points have for you as an individual and for you as an administrator? How might you put this learning to use outside the class?

Consider only what you have really learned. Don't try to figure out what other participants say they learned, or what you think you should have learned. If you feel you didn't learn anything, think about why. What could you have done to get more out of the exercise? How might the exercise have been structured differently to provide a better learning experience? What could be done in later exercises to help make them better learning experiences?

119

E.   Selected Readings

Blake, R.R., and Mouton, J.S., *The New Managerial Grid* (Houston: Gulf Publishing Co., 1978).

Fiedler, F.E., and Chemers, M.M., *Leadership and Effective Management* (Glenview, Ill.:   Scott, Foresman and Co., 1974).

Filley, A.C., House, R.J., and Kerr, S., *Managerial Process and Organizational Behavior*, 2d. ed., (Glenview, Ill.:   Scott, Foresman and Co., 1976), ch. 11, "Leadership: trait and behavioral approaches," and 12, "Leadership: situational approaches."

Glueck, W.F., *Management* (Hinsdale, Ill.:   The Dryden Press, 1977), ch. 7, "Leadership of employees."

Hersey, P., and Blanchard, K.H., *Management of Organizational Behavior*, 3d ed. (Englewood Cliffs, N.J.:   Prentice-Hall, 1977).

McGregor, D., *The Human Side of Enterprise* (New York: McGraw-Hill, 1960).

Starling, G., *Managing the Public Sector* (Homewood, Ill.:   The Dorsey Press, 1977), ch. 12, "Human behavior in organizations."

F. Participant Roles

S T O P!

Do Not Turn To The Next Page

The following pages contain descriptions of roles for the dean, chairpersons, and coordinators in this exercise.

Your instructor will assign *one* role to each individual and will tell you the page on which your role appears.

It is very important that you read *only* your own role prior to the exercise. Wait to read the other roles and follow-up comments until you have completed the exercise.

You Are On Your Honor!

Dean Leslie Pushin

You are dean of instructional operations at Greater Area Community College. You know that it is the policy of this institution to encourage decision making at the lowest possible level. But time and time again you have seen decisions made very badly, or not at all. You have therefore decided to "lead" this group to a decision which you believe is correct, without seeming to "tell" them. You privately believe that both of the two new positions should be given to the Paradental/Paramedical Department because this career field is going to explode in the next few years — and GACC must have sufficient staff in this department to anticipate and plan for expansion of evening and vocational programs.

Call the meeting to order and lead the group to the conclusion that the Paradental/Paramedical Department should get the two new positions without letting them know that you have already made up your mind.

Dean Leslie Leavit

You are dean of instructional operations at Greater Area Community College. Your style as dean has been to let the college run itself. You have no interest in forcing your will on responsible adults who know more about their own duties than you do. Besides, it is the policy of this institution to encourage decision making at the lowest possible level. You believe that professionals can and should act on the basis of their intrinsic values and their unique abilities to chart a path into an unknown future. All of your previous attempts to "manage" professional subordinates have ended in disastrous in-fighting and political upheaval. You have learned your lesson. Hands off!

For these reasons, give your group complete discretion in making a decision about the two new positions. You should call the meeting to order but should not intrude on the decision process.

Dean Leslie Helpem

You are dean of instructional operations at Greater Area Community College. You have been an avid student of educational administration and have learned that serious problems can result if a leader attempts to impose decisions on professionals without having given them an opportunity to consider the alternatives. You are fully aware of and in agreement with the policy of this institution to encourage decision making at the lowest possible level. On the other hand, you know that complete abdication of your responsibility for decision making, even if it is in the name of preserving professional autonomy, can lead to chaos, totally unacceptable decisions, or failure to make any decisions at all.

In view of these beliefs, help your group to attain an equitable, feasible and effective solution in this meeting. You must ensure that a decision is reached and that all parties accept the decision and are at least satisfied that all relevant issues have been discussed. You must also be sure that the decision is compatible with the goals of the college and provides clear encouragement for effective performance by chairpersons and faculty in the future.

Jo

You are the chairperson of the Electronics Department. You believe, and have always believed, that vocational education is the bread and butter of community colleges, and that it constitutes the primary reason for their existence. You have had the feeling for some years that "new and innovative" programs have drained heavily on voc-ed resources—in the name of something-for-everybody. The situation has been made worse by a destructive shift in faculty teaching loads. Voc-ed faculty in general, and faculty in your department in particular, have much heavier teaching loads than in the academic and service programs. It isn't fair!

You have been a department chairperson longer than any of the others at this meeting, and you have seen these issues beaten to death—without productive consequences. As a result, you are somewhat cynical about the purpose of the meeting. The current is moving in the direction of new things, new faces, new programs. You have recently undergone surgery and it has left you tired and lacking energy to tilt against windmills.

But there *is* a chance that you might be able to secure at least one new position if you argue persuasively at this meeting. You owe that to your faculty. Besides, you can legitimately claim that electronics is not just for majors preparing for entry-level jobs. It is for all levels, for transfer to four-year institutions, for enrichment of educational opportunities of nonmajors, and for development of many skills such as drafting. Well, here we go again!

Chris

You are coordinator of adult education at GACC. You regard this meeting with suspicion. It won't be the first time that you have been asked to "participate" in staffing decisions, but you have always suspected this is for show. The decisions never seem to go your way, and the result has been the belief by the whole Community Education Division that you are lowest on the totem pole. After all, you are different! Programs frequently happen off-campus; they are short courses which do not lead to degrees and are not embedded in the "academic" environment; you utilize evening instruction much more than other divisions; and most of all, your programs are directly tested by the marketplace. If each individual class or conference doesn't have a good reputation and a good sales pitch, it won't have students. No required courses here to protect your resource base.

On the other hand, you believe that adult education is the wave of the future. No college is going to be able to survive financially if it does not meet the *total* needs of its community. Adults have needs for education and reeducation that are at least as pressing as the needs of college-age youth. You need these two positions to secure the future of the college, to tap additional sources of outside funding, and to meet your present commitments. More importantly, you need to establish your right to have an important voice in decision making around here, for yourself *and* as a representative of Community Education. You wonder if the meeting will be dominated by Kelly's pitch for the college-transfer mission and the on-going squabble between Jo and Brett over new versus traditional vocational education. Here's hoping!

123

Brett

You are chairperson of the Paradental/Paramedical Department. As "new kid on the block," responsible for a new package of vocational education programs, the prospect of this meeting is ominous. The other people at this meeting are, by and large, old hands. They understand the political and budgeting structures of the college and state much better than you do. Furthermore, you know Jo will argue strongly that *traditional* voc-ed, with a documented history of success, should be emphasized. Kelly will stand up for the academic, college-transfer mission of the college, and Chris will do the same old song and dance about not having enough voice in decision making around here.

You have put your heart and soul into the development of health and health-related programs, and you believe that there is enormous potential in these career areas both in employment opportunities for your graduates and for generating new resources for the college. In fact, an off-hand remark by a member of your Advisory Committee has led you to believe that funding for these two new positions is somehow tied to the community's desire for more paraprofessional programs in health. Even though you have demonstrated the need for and success of these first paraprofessional programs, many people in other departments have expressed doubt about further expansion. Well, one thing is clear! If you don't get new contracted faculty positions, there isn't going to be any possibility of expansion. The planning and start-up activities are incredibly time-consuming. As a matter of fact, you may not even be able to maintain the present programs without new staffing. But health careers are "where the action is"!

Lynn

You are chairperson of the Mathematics Department. You heard about the impending meeting a week ago, and you had a good laugh with your faculty. You figure that the dean has already made up his mind about which department should get the two new positions but has called the meeting to preserve the appearance of democracy. In a way, you hope that's true, because if he hasn't, the group will *never* reach a decision. Jo and Brett will argue about "new-style" and "old-style" voc-ed; Chris will complain about being the forgotten division; and Kelly will carry the banner for academic courses. It is all a farce, and you have better things to do with your time.

But, on second thought, maybe Kelly could use some help. And what if, by some remote chance, it really is an open decision. The Math Department certainly needs new staffing to develop individualized instructional packages. There is such wide variation in the rate of learning of the many kinds of students who take math courses.

Maybe you'd better go to the meeting after all. It will be embarrasing to walk in because they are not expecting you. You could say something like, "Had a meeting cancelled at the last minute." Gulp! Here goes.

Kelly

You are chairperson of the Language Arts Department, and you are worried. It isn't easy to be the symbol of what's wrong with American youth. Every time someone asks you why Johnny can't read and write, you cringe. You think of the hundreds of students assigned to you for one or two semesters—to correct verbal deficiencies built up over students' lifetimes, inside and outside the classroom. You also supervise a diverse and expanding program in communication and foreign language. You must deal with constant pressure from the Office of Instruction to maintain high levels of student FTE. The future looks bleak indeed if society's expectation of full literacy is to be met.

In recent years, you have experimented successfully with teaching innovations such as individualized learning packages. These techniques and more will be required to meet the demand for academic transfer programs and service courses. Class sizes in English composition and literature are already out of hand. It is not just numbers in the classroom; it is also the grading and tutorial problem. No multiple choice tests here. Johnny and Suzie are supposed to be learning to write.

You look forward with eagerness to this meeting. You will argue that both faculty positions should be given to language arts—and you are determined to make your colleagues understand the importance of written and verbal communication. But you suspect that most of the meeting will be taken up with Jo and Brett arguing about "traditional" versus "new-fangled" vocational education, and Chris pleading for somebody to *listen* to the needs of the adult community. You believe these are much less important issues than the need to ensure that every graduate of GACC can read, write, and communicate. Besides, you need to protect the college-transfer mission of this college.

125

Follow-up Comments

Participative decision making has become, in recent years, an all-purpose prescription for organizational improvement. (It should be noted in passing that the word *delegation* has been around for a long time; the idea is hardly a new one.) Participative decision making is consistent with the principles of democracy and the full utilization of managerial and worker skills. Its benefits are heralded as the pathway to organizational commitment, job enrichment, morale building and, not least of all, better decisions. The last factor, better decisions, depends on the assumption that the people who do particular tasks in an organization are the very people who know their tasks the best and are thus equipped with the knowledge and skills to make their own decisions.

The exercise you have just completed has been carefully constructed to stack all the cards against you. Role conflicts were intentionally induced; no provision was made for training and preparation of group members; no consideration was given to environmental needs (survival of the college) or identification of superordinate objectives. In some of the roles, a negative and cynical mind set was deliberately conveyed. No attention was given to the very real anxiety on the part of most managers that nobody will pay any attention to their decisions, let alone implement them.

So it is not surprising that this exercise frequently results in bad decisions, no decision at all, dissatisfaction, and embarrassment or hostility on the part of the role players. If this were the real world, we would expect other negative consequences to crop up next week and next year.

How to do it right if you are the leader of participative decision making? *Prepare* participators by providing needed information, skills training in group processes, and a clear understanding of the desired outcome: deliberation, recommendation, or decision. *Identify* decisions that are most in need of acceptance by members of the organization and that require the knowledge of participators (use participative management sparingly and wisely; it is a time-consuming and sensitive process). *Set superordinate objectives* to which all members of the decision-making team can ascribe, thus to provide some basis for agreement. *Acknowledge* the existence of incompatible objectives and the reality of scarce resources. Focus on creative ways to turn a zero-sum, win-lose circumstance into win-win. *Set criteria* by which the decision is to be made before making the decision (this factor is probably the least obvious, most important, and least practiced element of decision making, individual or group). *Evaluate* both the process and the outcome of the decision-making task. How could we have done it better? What should we do differently next time?

A final note: If the size of your class was sufficient to use all three dean's roles, you may notice some interesting differences in the satisfaction and performance of the groups. The role written for Dean Helpem, a facilitor, is clearly more consistent with the intent of participative decision making. Consider the implications if the group leader adopts a posture of manipulator (Pushin) or abdicator (Leavitt) and then asks his or her subordinates to "participate in making an important decision."

EXERCISE 11

Employee Motivation in Public Agencies

Purpose

1. To understand the preferences employees express for various job characteristics.
2. To compare patterns in what people express as their own preferences for job characteristics to what they think are other people's preferences.
3. To develop an appreciation for the impact on managers' behaviors of their assumptions about other persons' work preferences.
4. To expose participants to alternative administrative approaches to enhancing employee productivity through their personal motivations.

Preparation

None.

Group Size

Any size.

Time Requirement

Minimum of seventy-five minutes.

Physical Setting

None.

Related Issues

Work ethic and other work values, management styles, employee satisfaction, employee productivity.

129

A.   Introduction

Much of the job of public management involves influencing others to expend energy in the pursuit of agency or public goals. Where much of the work is done by people as opposed to machines, as in government services, the problem of effectively carrying out this influencing looms extra large. In addition, this issue is important because citizens are demanding more or better services from government for the same or fewer taxes. This desired increase in the productivity of government can largely come only from the increased effectiveness of government employees. Thus, understanding public employee motivation is necessary for the public manager of the 1980s, as a way for him or her to affect civil servants' individual and collective productivity.

Motivation is a complex and dynamic function. It concerns the releasing of effort in the pursuit of particular purposes or goals. Of course, it is not a simple or fixed human quality that can be easily turned on or off. There exists no single, magic technique that administrators can use to tap into employee motivation. Furthermore, some of the traditional methods seem to be losing their efficacy.

And, yet, in the end, administrators cannot accomplish the complex tasks placed before their public agencies unless they are able to motivate other civil servants to work at their fullest potential. Only then is it possible to direct them toward achievement of the goals that have been established for the agency or body of government by policymakers.

Success or failure in the provision of government services is only partially dependent on the technical expertise of the administrator. Much of the success or failure depends on the administrator's understanding of the people surrounding his or her position. This statement is not meant to denigrate the need to understand the various skills essential to the operation of a modern government. But influencing others to use those skills remains a paramount concern. For example, city managers are seldom released from their positions because they lack technical skills. They can buy the necessary accounting, planning, or public health skills. City managers usually lose their jobs because they do not know how to get along with city employees, city council members, or the local constituent groups, such as the neighborhood associations or the businessmen's clubs. Similarly, complaints registered against employees working within the bureaucracy are usually not complaints about the lack of expertise. Instead, the complaints deal with the way other employees, or the public, are treated by the person against whom the complaint is lodged. This has also been true when employees have complained about the way managers have handled them. It is human relations skills which are among the most important tools required for a public administrator to be successful.

An important step in becoming a successful public manager is to develop an understanding of motivation, which is that force within individuals that incites or impels them to action. This exercise provides a way to examine your assumptions about what motivates people—including yourself—and to compare those assumptions to what people say about their own sources of motivation.

B. Procedure

1. Table 11.1 lists five factors that are often thought to motivate performance in organizations. Rank the five factors from the strongest to the weakest motivators of performance for each of the job-holders described on page 132, as well as for yourself. Place a value of 1 on those factors considered to be most important to the individual and a value of 5 on those considered to be least important (*fifteen minutes*).

TABLE 11.1

Motivation Factors	Jobholders			
	Administrator	Secretary	Warehouseworker	You
High income				
No danger of being fired				
Short work hours and much free time				
Chances for advancement				
Important and meaningful work				

Jobholders

Administrator, Statsville Health Department. Supervises and directs the efforts of a team of ten public health inspectors.

Secretary to the administrator, Statsville Health Department. Performs typing, stenographic, and related secretarial services.

Warehouseworker, Statsville Roads and Maintenance Department. Removes cartons and other deliveries from the dock, puts them where they belong in the warehouse, and keeps necessary records.

2. Next, the instructor should reproduce the table on a blackboard or large piece of paper. Make a frequency count of the factors that are ranked 1 for each jobholder. This can be done most easily by the instructor. If each participant will repeat to the instructor the numbers of the four factors which are ranked 1 for each of the respective jobholders, then the instructor can place a mark in the necessary spaces of the table. The resulting frequency count will provide a profile of the responses of the class to the assumed motivation factors (*fifteen minutes*).

3. What meaning does the class see in these data? The following questions may help guide this discussion (*twenty minutes*).
    a. Is there any consensus in what is assumed to motivate other people?
    b. Is there a consistency in responses as to what motivates the participants themselves?
    c. What is the relation between what participants presume motivates others and what they say about themselves? Is there any? Why or why not?
    d. How many empty spaces are there in the table? What does that mean?
    e. Do assumptions about what motivates other persons relate to individual managerial style? What if the assumptions are not accurate?
    f. Would any single focus for a program to motivate others be effective for this group of participants? Would flexibility make more sense?

4. The instructor will read to the class the percentages of workers, selecting each motivational factor as most important to them. The percentages should be recorded in Table 11.2. These data are derived from longitudinal surveys being carried out by the U.S. government

TABLE 11.2   *What Workers Want from Their Jobs*

Motivational Factor	Type of Worker							
	Professional/ Technical	Managerial/ Administrative	Clerical	Craft	Operative	Transport Equipment Operator and Labor (Excluding Farm)	Farm	Service Worker
High income								
No danger of being fired								
Short work hours and much free time								
Chances for advancement								
Important and meaningful work								

and reported in C.N. Weaver, "What Workers Want From Their Jobs."* Numerous other researchers and organizations have found similar results (see selected readings)(*five minutes*).

5. What meaning does the class see in table 11.2? The following questions may help focus this discussion (*twenty minutes*):
    a. Which box in each column contains the largest percentage of responses? Is this surprising? Why or why not?
    b. What difference does it make that most (though, clearly, not all) persons rank a particular factor as 1? What difference does it make that it is that particular factor?

*Adapted, by permission of the publisher, from "What Workers Want From Their Jobs," by C.N. Weaver, *Personnel*, May-June 1976. ©1976 by AMACOM, a division of American Management Associations, pp. 48-54. All rights reserved.

   c. What difference does it make that many persons rank *other* factors as 1, that is, that there is no stronger agreement among individuals? Again, would a single motivation program work for any given category of workers?

   d. Given high degrees of difference between individual employees, how can an administrator design programs and an organization to be flexible and, thus, effectively deal with this reality?

6. (*For the instructor only*).
    The following numbers are the percentages of workers who chose each motivational factor to be most important to them. They are listed so as to fill in each column in Table I, from top to bottom. Read them to the class to fill in their Tables during Step 4 of the exercise. P/T: 8, 3, 4, 14, 71; M/A: 15, 1, 4, 19, 60; C: 22, 13, 2, 24, 39; Cr: 18, 14, 8, 14, 46; Op: 17, 11, 5, 31, 36; TEO&L: 29, 8, 6, 17, 40; F: 22, 9, 0, 17, 52; SW: 7, 7, 7, 22, 58.

C. Assessment of Learning

Think about what you have done in this exercise. Try to identify two or three major points that you have learned from this experience. What meaning do these points have for you as an individual and for you as an administrator? How might you put this learning to use outside the class?

      Consider only what you have really learned. Don't try to figure out what other participants say they learned, or what you think you should have learned. If you feel you didn't learn anything, think about why. What could you have done to get more out of the exercise? How might the exercise have been structured differently to provide a better learning experience? What could be done in later exercises to help make them better learning experiences?

D. Selected Readings

Briscoe, D.R., *101 Ways to Motivate Employees* (San Diego: Management and Personnel Systems, 1979).

Dowling, W.F., and Sayles, L.R., *How Managers Motivate*, 2d ed. (New York: McGraw-Hill, 1978).

Gellerman, S.W., *Motivation and Productivity* (New York: American Management Association, 1963).

Katz, D., and Kahn, R.L., *The Social Psychology of Organizations*, 2d ed. (New York: John Wiley and Sons, 1978).

Katzell, R.A., Yankelovich, D., et al. *Work, Productivity, and Job Satisfaction* (New York: The Psychological Corporation, 1975).

Meyers, M.S., *Every Employee a Manager* (New York: McGraw-Hill, 1970).

Schaeffer, S.D., *The Motivation Process* (Cambridge, Mass.: Winthrop Publishers, 1977).

Yankelovich, D., "The new psychological contracts at work," *Psychology Today*, May 1978, 46–50.

SECTION
D

Intraagency Relations:
The Problems of Communications

EXERCISE 12

A Single Organization with Several Minds: Writing Regulations

Purpose

1. To experience the problems that emerge in interactions among the departments of the same agency when those departments have different primary goals.
2. To demonstrate the effects on work accomplished, agency procedures, and the pursuit of multiple goals of decision making that requires communication among different departments when compared with decision making by individuals.
3. To demonstrate the number of factors that an agency must take into account when writing regulations and to participate in a limited regulation writing exercise.
4. To indicate the extensive costs associated with implementing individual regulations and the relationships between those costs and the benefits of implementation.

Preparation

Students who are not familiar with the *Federal Register* and the regulations for federal grant programs should locate one or more copies in a library or in the office of an agency which uses them and spend at least an hour reading them in order to become familiar with the form, language, and content of the sections relevant to this exercise (general provisions, grant administration, etc.).

Group Size

Seven minimum. Any larger number can participate. The instructor may want to divide a very large class into smaller groups for step 5 of the procedure.

Time Requirement

Ninety minutes to two hours minimum class time. The instructor may wish to devote additional class time as discussed under the procedure. Approximately four hours of out-of-class work are also required.

A. Introduction

For exercise 5, you prepared a grant proposal for funds to establish a drug abuse center for veterans. The U.S. Department of Health, Education and Welfare (HEW) was the agency to which the proposal was submitted. In this exercise you will switch roles and become employees of the funding agency, HEW. You will be responsible for writing some of the regulations that will govern the use of the funds. The exercise will help you consider a number of phenomena: the relative clarity and ease of implementation of regulations written by individuals and by groups; the impact of technical and political constraints on regulation writing and program implementation; the potential costs to agencies and taxpayers of the regulations imposed on government programs.

Every participant works for a division of HEW that administers programs which try to help persons overcome their drug abuse problems. The class instructor is the director of the division. The Secretary of HEW, at the suggestion of some of her top advisers and other outside interests, has transferred some of the money in HEW's budget from other activities to drug abuse activities. The Secretary has instructed the director of your division to develop regulations for a drug abuse program that will serve segments of the population which do not receive adequate service from existing programs. In the Secretary's directive the kind of drug abuse program is not specified, and "segments of the population" and "adequate service" are not defined.

The director decides to test the relative merits of two approaches to writing regulations: the traditional system of having each office within the division take part so that the interests, activities, and problems of each are considered, and the use of a single adviser to write the complete set of regulations. Concern in both cases is to produce regulations that are clearly written and easily understood, cover all necessary points and contingencies, and impose no unnecessary administrative costs. The director instructs all of those who work on the regulations to include a requirement that all proposals be submitted for A-95 clearinghouse review. (See exercise 5, section A, if you are unfamiliar with A-95 review.)

The students will be assigned to write regulations either individually, as special assistants to the director of the division, or as members of teams representing different offices within the division. The regulations will be written outside class; they will be compared and discussed during class.

Steps 1, 6, and 7 will be completed in class. Step 2 may be completed in class.

B. Procedure

1. Assign and review roles and establish time table (*ten minutes*). The instructor will establish deadlines for the completion of steps 2, 3, and 4. The three teams in each set of teams must complete their initial drafts in time to meet together to prepare a final draft for the director.

2. The student teams meet separately to prepare draft regulations; the student(s) serving as special assistant(s) to the director prepare their drafts individually, without help from other students. The subjects of the regulations to be written by each are listed in section F. Note that the definition of terms, including "adequate service" and eligible "segments of the population," is a very important part of the regulation writing process (*two hour maximum*).

3. Each set of student teams (one team from each office) meets together to prepare its report to the director. The report will consist of a cover memorandum and the proposed regulations. The teams are expected to integrate their suggestions into a single coherent package (coherent in terms of language and definitions of terms, goals, and objectives), not simply to staple their three separate draft reports together (*two hour maximum*).

4. Reports are submitted to the director before class so that he or she may review them and point out any differences between those prepared by groups and those prepared by individuals. Differences may appear in length, clarity, coherence, style, complexity, political savvy, level of technical competence required for implementation, etc.

5. Discussion (*about two hours*).

141

C. Discussion and Conclusions

1. The instructor will identify differences in the following character-
    istics of the regulations submitted by different groups and individ-
    uals:

    length
    clarity
    coherence
    style
    complexity
    political savvy
    technical competence required for implementation

    How did group versus individual authorship affect each of these
    characteristics? What was the impact on the final product of the
    rivalries and different primary interests which characterize different
    offices within the same agency?

2. Given the many purposes served by regulations, which is the better
    way to have them prepared—by an individual or by a committee?

3. What lessons about intraagency relations (those between different
    offices within the same agency) can be drawn from your experience
    with this exercise? What is the role and importance of communica-
    tion in these relations?

4. What differences and similarities do you perceive between intra-
    organizational and interorganizational relations?

5. What adjectives would you use to describe the regulations written
    by the agencies of the federal government? Why? What evidence, if
    any, do you have to show that your description is accurate?

The following topics are rarely considered by federal agencies during the regulation writing process, but they have very important implications for public managers. Unfortunately there are no available models to use for the cost-benefit analysis of individual regulations.

6. Identify the costs to the grant-receiving agencies of implementing the regulations that the class has written. Costs will include at least the staff time that will be required for record keeping and filing reports, but may also include staff time spent resolving political problems created by the definition of client groups or other provisions, supply and equipment costs, etc.

7. Although the class cannot attach absolute dollar amounts to any particular cost, discuss ranges of dollar amounts for staff time, computerized versus manual record keeping, etc., in order to begin to understand how costly the implementation of regulations can be.

8. Identify the benefits associated with each of the costs and compare who benefits with who bears the costs. Are the costs warranted by the benefits?

D.   Assessment of Learning

Think about what you have done in this exercise. Try to identify two or three major points that you have learned from this experience. What meaning do these points have for you as an individual and for you as an administrator? How might you put this learning to use outside the class?

Consider only what you have really learned. Don't try to figure out what other participants say they learned, or what you think you should have learned. If you feel you didn't learn anything, think about why. What could you have done to get more out of the exercise? How might the exercise have been structured differently to provide a better learning experience? What could be done in later exercises to help make them better learning experiences?

E.   Selected Readings

Luft, J., *Group Processes*, 2d ed. (Palo Alto, Calif.:   Mayfield Publishing Co., 1970).

Rogers, E.M., and Agarwala-Rogers, R., *Communication in   nizations* (New York: The Free Press, 1976).

Schein, E.H., *Process Consultation* (Reading, Mass.:   son-Wesley, 1969).

F.   Participant Roles

Students assigned to:

1. The Policy Office will draft the regulations that articulate goals and objectives and that specify eligible client groups. The primary concern of members of this office is the adoption of policies that satisfy the political constituencies of the division, including the Secretary of HEW and the agency's many clients, all of whom always seem to want more program resources. You want to offer something to everyone.

2. The Program Office will draft the regulations that establish procedures for disbursing funds and for monitoring and evaluation of program operation. (Note: You will not be writing procedures for program operation; this will not be a complete set of regulations.) The primary concern of members of this office is generating information which can be used to impress Congress and the Secretary. This means that you want to concentrate use of resources in the hands of a few groups so that large, clearly measurable results are achieved. This also means that you want grantees to submit narrative reports that describe successful programs in detail.

3. The Budget Office will draft the regulations that establish record-keeping requirements and procedures for reporting, auditing, and avoiding misspending. The primary concern of members of this office is to avoid the public embarrass-

ment to the agency that accompanies disclosures of misuse of public funds. This means that you want grantees to keep extensive financial records that present receipts and expenditures and services delivered in the most concise way possible.

Each team should consist of at least two but not more than five members. There may be more than one set of teams, but there should be the same number of teams representing each office. Each set of teams (one team representing each office) will submit a separate report to the director.

The instructor will also assign one or more students to serve as special assistants to the director. There should be at least one special assistant for each set of teams, but there may be more. Each special assistant will write regulations covering all of the topics required for the three offices listed immediately above and will submit a separate report (cover memo and draft regulations) to the director. The primary concern of the special assistant(s) is to improve the efficiency of the division and its grant implementation system.

PART
III

Management Of Public Agencies

PART III Management of Public Agencies

The exercises in Part III involve students in a number of the tasks of management common to both public and private organizations. The skills learned are among those traditionally taught in schools of business administration but only recently introduced into the training of public administrators. Exercise 13 requires students to develop a PERT/Time Network, a tool useful in grantwriting as well as other planning activities. Decision making is the focus of exercises 14 and 15, demonstrating the effects of and ways to deal with value conflicts among individuals involved in a single decision process and requiring the prioritization of activities by a manager faced with more demands than can be met in a given period of time. Exercise 16 illustrates the complexities and difficulties associated with the evaluation of public organizations and programs and involves students in the use of some evaluation tools. Exercises 17 and 18 involve students in the budgetary process, both in choosing the kind of budget best suited for an agency's needs and in allocating available funds among alternative uses. Finally, exercises 19 and 20 involve students in two areas of particular concern to public personnel administrators and to all managers who must live with the results of the work of personnel departments: affirmative action and negotiating a union contract.

SECTION
A

Planning

EXERCISE 13
Planning for the Veterans' Drug Abuse Center

Purpose

To gain experience in the use of a specialized planning tool: the PERT/Time Network.

Preparation

Read the introduction and complete step 1 of the procedure before class.

Group Size

Any size.

Time Requirement

One hour and fifty minutes.

Physical Setting:

Blackboard (also, a room with chairs that will enable students to work in small groups, if step 3 is undertaken by small groups).

Related Issues

Grant writing, decision making, time management, prioritizing, and objective setting.

A. Introduction

In exercise 5 your class produced one or more proposals for a grant that would be used to establish and run a Veterans' Drug Abuse Center. In exercise 12, you helped write regulations for the program. Regardless of

151

the outcome of exercise 5 and the recommendation made by its A-95 clearinghouse, you are now to assume that the proposal was approved for funding by HEW.

Now you are to assume the role of the person who has responsibility for planning the implementation of the program. You must identify the principal tasks which must be undertaken before the first year of the program ends, including the initial annual audit of the program you will decide what will be done when.

To help you organize your thinking and to provide a framework for your implementation plan, you will develop a PERT/Time Network for the program's first year. Doing so organizes your thinking and enables you to plan for the myriad of small tasks without losing sight of the program's objectives and time constraints.

Your list of objectives and of tasks to be completed during the first year must include not only management tasks (hiring personnel, establishing office space and information systems, monitoring, evaluating, auditing, etc.) but should also consider the flow of services (when services will be provided to how many clients, etc.).

B. Procedure

1. Before class develop a PERT/Time Network for the first year's implementation of the grant for the Veterans' Drug Abuse Center. You must identify the principal tasks which must be undertaken in order to draw the network indicating both activities and events. Do *not* undertake the calculation of expected times by determining the distribution of shortest, longest, and most likely times. Instead, given the established one-year time frame and the list of principal tasks, assign reasonable amounts of the available time to the activities. Then locate the critical path and indicate it on your network drawing with double lines or a different color.

2. Under the leadership of the instructor, the class will pool the results of its individual efforts under step 1. First compile a list of principle tasks and then draw the PERT Network incorporating all of these tasks on the blackboard (*thirty minutes*).

3. This step may be completed by the entire class together or by any number of smaller groups designated by the instructor. Calculate the expected time of each activity. You may refer to any of the selected readings or other material on PERT while working on this step (*one hour*).

4. Discussion (*twenty minutes*).

C. Discussion and Conclusions

1. If you had used PERT during the initial writing of the grant proposal, would you have produced a better grant proposal? Why?

2. For what various planning tasks and situations would PERT be a useful tool? For what administrative tasks and situations?

3. How would you modify the PERT Network to make it more useful?

D. Assessment of Learning

Think about what you have done in this exercise. Try to identify two or three major points that you have learned from this experience. What meaning do these points have for you as an individual and for you as an administrator? How might you put this learning to use outside the class?

Consider only what you have really learned. Don't try to figure out what other participants say they learned, or what you think you should have learned. If you feel you didn't learn anything, think about why. What could you have done to get more out of the exercise? How might the exercise have been structured differently to provide a better learning experience? What could be done in later exercises to help make them better learning experiences?

153

E.   Selected Readings

For an easy to understand explanation of PERT, see Thierauf, Robert J., *An Intro-ductory Approach to Operations Research* (Santa Barbara, Calif.:   John Wiley and Sons, 1978).

Cabot, A.V., and Harnett, D.L., *An Introduction to Management Science* (Reading, Mass.:   Addison-Wesley, 1977), pp. 100–109.

Levin, R., and Kirkpatrick, C., *Planning and Control with PERT/CPM* (New York: McGraw-Hill, 1966).

Moder, J.J., and Phillips, C.R., *Project Management with CPM and PERT* (New York: Van Nostrand, 1970).

Thiel, H., Boot, J.C.G., and Klock, T., *Operations Research and Quantitative Economics: An Elementary Introduction* (New York: McGraw-Hill, 1975), ch. 2.

Wiest, J.D., and Levy, F.K., *A Management Guide to PERT/CPM* (Englewood Cliffs, N.J.:   Prentice-Hall, 1969).

SECTION
B

Decision-Making

EXERCISE 14

Values and Group Decision-Making: Choosing a Prime Sponsor Director

Purpose

1. To explore group choices that involve differing member values.
2. To explore factors affecting group decision making (social status, race, religion, sex, and many others).
3. To learn to solve group conflicts while making a decision.

Preparation

Read introduction, procedure, problem description and résumé data ahead of time. Background information on CETA is in appendix C.

Group Size

Small groups of seven. Additional participants can act as assistants to the primary seven role holders or as observers of group processes.

Time Requirement

One hour fifty minutes.

Physical Setting

A room with tables or movable chairs so that students can be organized into small groups.

This exercise was developed from "Values and Group Decision Making: The Layoff" by F.S. Hall, in *Experiences in Management and Organizational Behavior* by D.T. Hall, D.D. Bowen, R.J. Lewicki, and F.S. Hall. Copyright ©1975 John Wiley and Sons, Inc. Reprinted by permis- of John Wiley and Sons, Inc.

Related Issues

Power, leadership, interpersonal co   nunications, and organizational communications.

A.   Introduction

Many decisions in work organizations ɛ   de by groups. The degree of participation among group members ᵥ   om decision to decision, from group to group, and from orgaɪ   to organization. All situations not only involve the group men.   ʰnical expertise, but also their personal opinions and values. Tʰ   ᵒf conflict within the group is likely to be highly related to the   ʼ different value premises represented in the group. Groups that ᵤ   ᵉ on the outcome to be achieved will have difficulty in solᵥ   ᵉms and in making decisions.

Decisions based on the values of the members of ᵣ   roup are different from decisions based on organizational goals anɑ   ʲectives. They are more difficult to make and usually take much lonɡ   Group members are less likely to be influenced by an expert. They   ly less on information and accuracy and more on personal judgmen   per-ceptions, and emotions. Thus, group members may try to ᵥ   the decision rather than to seek the best possible solution for achieviₗ   ʈhe goals or objectives. And they are more likely to resort to bargaₗ   ₐg, voting, satisficing, or forming coalitions than to bringing all posᵢ   ʼe expertise to bear on the analysis of alternatives.

Organizations can minimize the effects of personal values in decision making by providing clear goals for administrators and work groups. They can train groups to first establish criteria that will guide the choices and actions of the group. In these ways, conflicts can be resolved, particularly when those conflicts arise from differing personal values among the group members.

B.   Procedure

In this exercise you are asked to make a decision that is not uncommon in government or the private sector, the selection of an administrator. The decision will involve a conflict of values of both the applicants for the position and of the selection committee.

In order to reach a decision the group should review each résumés discussing the positive and negative aspects of each of the applicants. The group should consider the applicants' grasps of the quantitative

Carol Thompson: Age thirty, American Indian. Currently unemployed. Previously served as liaison between American Indian movement and the Bureau of Indian Affairs in Washington, D.C.

Education: Attended two-year program at Chemeketa Community College. Received educational grant from the Bureau of Indian Affairs and graduated with human resource degree (B.S.) from New Mexico State.

Dave Williams: Age thirty nine, white. Four years with the U.S. Department of Labor in Washington, D.C.; associate professor in business at University of Montana; assistant professor, organizational behavior, at Big City State University.

Education: B.S. business, Washington State; M.S. public administration, University of South Carolina; Ph.D. organizational behavior, American University.

2. After everyone is familiar with the problem, all members of the group should briefly introduce themselves to the rest of the committee, explaining what group they represent, their occupation and perhaps interests. The group should then discuss the alternatives for the director's position until a consensus is reached on rankings. The group may not decide by a majority vote. Members must be given the chance to convince the rest of the group of their point of view. All group members must agree to the final decision. Record the time it takes you to reach a decision (*forty-five minutes*).

3. Each group will report on its decision-making processes and outcomes. The instructor will record the data on the board (*twenty minutes*).

4. Discussion (*thirty minutes*).

C. Discussion and Conclusions

1. How can a group keep value issues from affecting its decision making?

2. What happens in a group when its members make decisions on the basis of their individual values?

3. How can an organization reduce value conflicts in decision making?

4. How can work teams resolve or minimize the impact of value conflicts? What techniques might they use?

5. How do decisions involving values differ from decisions where there are objective, "right" answers?

D.   Assessment of Learning

Think about what you have done in this exercise. Try to identify two or three major points that you have learned from this experience. What meaning do these points have for you as an individual and for you as an administrator? How might you put this learning to use outside the class?

Consider only what you have really learned. Don't try to figure out what other participants say they learned, or what you think you should have learned. If you feel you didn't learn anything, think about why. What could you have done to get more out of the exercise? How might the exercise have been structured differently to provide a better learning experience? What could be done in later exercises to help make them better learning experiences?

E.   Selected Readings

Guth, W.D., and Taguiri, R., "Personal values and corporate strategy," *Harvard Business Review*, September/October 1965, 123–32.

Likert, R., and Likert, J.G., *New Ways of Managing Conflict* (New York: McGraw-Hill, 1976).

Robbins, S.P., *Managing Organizational Conflict* (Englewood Cliffs, N.J.:   Prentice-Hall, 1974).

F.   Participant Roles

Values and Group Decision-making Roles

Each of you has been given a role to play in the decision-making process. Before you begin discussing the candidates for the position of director, members of the group should introduce themselves to the rest of the group. You should reveal only the information in the character sketch and not the role you will play during the exercise.

In order for this to be a stimulating and educational exercise, it is important for each of you to become aware of the character you are representing. Think about how this person would respond to the various members of the group and also how he or she would view the resumes of the applicants for the position of director of the CVMC.

Sharon Smith: White, thirty-four years old. B.A. in sociology from University of Pacifica. Currently Polk County commissioner.

Sharon is divorced and has two young children. She was a caseworker for Children's Service Division but retired to serve full time on the County Commission. In her past work experiences she saw the value of providing an opportunity for meaningful employment and sees educational programs and on-the-job training as the best methods for achieving this goal.

Role: Sharon is willing to compromise on some issues. She looks at the applicants as individuals and how they can assist people and is not terribly interested in their educational background or previous job experiences.

Margaret Cole: White, fifty years old. M.S. in urban planning from the University of Pacifica; currently a manpower planner for CVMC.

Margaret is single; she has been in government employment for twenty-five years. Her interests are in equal opportunity employment and in feminist activities. She has been an officer in the Business and Professional Women for many years and is now on the board of directors of the YWCA.

Role: Margaret is outspoken, very firm in her beliefs, and is considered very liberal in her thinking. She would be willing to experiment with new techniques in the employment field and would be interested in having a director who reflects her attitudes.

George Silvers: White, forty-five years old. B.A. (at thirty) from California State and M.A. from University of San Francisco in journalism.

George has been a teacher for fifteen years; is currently a member of the Board of Education in Capital City. He is married, his wife is a junior high teacher. They have two boys, twenty three and twenty one—one in college and one in the navy.

163

Role: Autocratic. George is very outspoken, doesn't beat around the bush, grew up in the school of hard knocks, and either has friends or enemies—nothing in between. Understands how to play the bureaucracy game to receive more funding.

John Bates: White, forty-four years old. B.A. from University of Pacifica in business. Currently county commissioner of Yamhill County.

John is the president of a local bank and is very active in the community and in his church; he is head of a youth weekend athletic program. Married with two children.

Role: John tends to be democratic but is also used to having his opinion carry quite a bit of weight. He also has more status within the group because of his elected position and also because of his financial position.

Debbie Mertz: White, thirty-seven years old.

Debbie is married, the mother of three children and is a homemaker. She is currently the president of the elementary school PTA, the chairperson of the Community Theater Group, and a Blue Bird leader. Debbie served as the county coordinator for the George Wallace for President campaign in the last election and is serving on CVMC committee as member-at-large.

Role: Opinionated, prejudiced, and outspoken. Places a great deal of value on appearances and affluence.

Steve Amos: Black, thirty-two years old. B.A. and M.A. from Stanford University in management and administration.

Steve is currently a planner for the Central Valley Manpower Consortium; he is a former coordinator for the Informational Referral and Outreach Program in Polk County. Steve is married and has four children; his wife, Kate Amos, is the county director of Equal Rights for Women. Steve is a native of Pacifica and has been very active in various youth programs such as the Job Corps.

Role: Conservative thinker, quiet and passive. Will tend to be a compromiser and will work to achieve harmony within the group.

Jim Pierce: White, forty-two years old.

Jim has only high school education but through hard work has become the owner of a very successful trucking business. Jim is married and has three teenage sons. One of Jim's major concerns has been the employment of young people. Jim is the Marion County commissioner on the CVMC committee.

Role: Jim is very conservative. He has a blue-collar background and is concerned about providing deserving male youth and male heads of households with

164

good jobs. He does not want to create public sector make-work jobs. He is a blocker in group discussions and trains his thoughts on only certain topics. He interrupts quite often to make his point.

EXERCISE 15

Problems in Administration of Employment and Training Programs: An In-Basket Exercise

Purpose

1. To create a realistic and stressful administrative, decision-making situation.
2. To provide practice in making administrative decisions in a CETA prime sponsor's office.
3. To expand the individual's awareness of his/her administrative tendencies as well as of decision alternatives and implications.

Preparation

Read the introduction and procedure. Background information on CETA is in appendix C.

Group Size

Any size.

Time Requirement

Approximately two hours. The discussion phase could involve more time, depending on the purposes of the instructor.

Physical Setting

No special setting needed.

Related Issues

Time management, delegation, leadership style, decision making, prioritizing and objective setting, organizational politics.

A.   Introduction

The other exercises in this booklet have involved role playing, face-to-face interactions, and simulated group situations. The in-basket exercise is designed to reveal how participants handle real management problems on their own. The in-basket is an exercise which uses a simulated organizational setting and a series of hypothetical incidents. It offers a series of situations or problems which each participant must analyze to prepare a solution. These solutions are then shared during group discussion so that each participant can compare his/her answers with those of others.

Generally, this exercise looks at how individuals approach administrative work, including the overall organization of work, priority setting, and the handling of interrelationships among situations. Also examined are written communication skills, human relations skills, creativity, tendency to seek approval from others for actions, individual work standards, tolerance of uncertainty, resistance to stress, degree of personal and work energy, organization and planning procedures, and personal decision-making techniques.

The appendix to this exercise provides a suggested procedure for analyzing participants' handling of this in-basket exercise. Often this type of exercise is used to evaluate the administrative behaviors of potential and current administrators. The appendix includes a procedure for such an analysis.

B.   Procedure

Your assignment is to read all of the documents in the in-basket, as well as the list of things to do that you brought back from Washington, D.C., and to indicate what you will do with or about each one (the list of things to do brought from Washington, D.C. appears at the end of the items in the in-basket). Answer the following questions about each item:

What action is called for?

How urgent is it?

When will you carry it out (in relation to the other tasks that must be done)?

What are the political implications of the decision you must make?

What conflict, if any, does the document present between your short-term interests and expediency and your long-term interests?

168

We are interested in how you will organize your time as well as what you will do. You may record your answers to these questions about each document on the document.

Once you have decided what to do in response to each document, you are to proceed to the set of questions which appears in the discussion and conclusions section. Do not read these questions until after you have completed your consideration of the individual items in the in-basket. Much of the self-learning that should emerge from your participation in this exercise may be lost if you read the questions first, for they may guide your responses regarding the individual documents.

In the class discussion, individual students will be expected to compare their own decisions with those generally agreed on by the class as most acceptable or useful. The purpose of the entire exercise is to expand student awareness of their own particular administrative tendencies and to expand awareness of the implications and possible alternatives to individual administrative decisions.

Before proceeding with the exercise, reread the scenario above at least one more time. Be sure you understand your situation and expectations before beginning to read the in-basket. After you have read the in-basket, be sure you have provided the requested information for each document before proceeding to section C.

C. Discussion and Conclusions

These questions are to be answered individually prior to group discussion.

1. How did you "attack" the documents?
    a. Did you respond to the materials in their original sequence or did you go to the bottom of the pile and start from there? How many of the documents did you read from the top before going to the bottom?
    b. Did you sort the items?
    c. Did you respond to all the items? If not, why?
    d. What method(s) of delegation did you use?
    e. Did you make final decisions, hold for further information, postpone, etc.?

2. Identify your immediate problems requiring rapid solution; list them in the order they should be attacked.

3. Identify your long-term problems and list them in order of importance

4. Do the solutions for these various problems conflict? That is, does the solution of one problem promise to make another problem worse? Identify the conflicts and how you will resolve them.

5. Explain what you hope to accomplish by noon, February 19.

6. Explain how you expect to accomplish these things. How will you handle specific tasks and problems?

7. How would your response to Ted and the apparent interpersonal problems in your office differ: (1) if you were aware of the problems before you left for Washington, D.C.? (2) if you were not aware of the problems before you left?

8. Identify the political alliances in your environment which you must deal with and indicate how they relate to each other.

D. Assessment of Learning

Think about what you have done in this exercise. Try to identify two or three major points that you have learned from this experience. What meaning do these points have for you as an individual and for you as an administrator? How might you put this learning to use outside the class?

Consider only what you have really learned. Don't try to figure out what other participants say they learned, or what you think you should have learned. If you feel you didn't learn anything, think about why. What could you have done to get more out of the exercise? How might the exercise have been structured differently to provide a better learning experience? What could be done in later exercises to help make them better learning experiences?

E. Selected Readings

Bray, D.W., Campbell, R.J., and Grant, D.L., *Formative Years in Business* (New York: John Wiley and Sons, 1974).

DuBrin, A.J., *The Practice of Managerial Psychology* (Elmsford, N.Y.: Pergamon Press, 1972).

Joyce, R.D., "In-basket programs," *Training in Business and Industry*, February 1971.

Leavitt, H.J., *Managerial Psychology* (Chicago: University of Chicago Press, 1972).

F. Working Documents

Problem Statement

You are to assume the role of Robert Max, staff director of the Brownsville Manpower Planning Office. The mayor and CETA prime sponsor, Norman Nile, appointed you staff director as a reward for your service as youth organizer for his previous campaign. Brownsville has a population of 847,000. The mayor challenged the machine of his own party to win the primary in the previous election and went on to win the general election by only 1,300 votes. The machine continues to distrust him and is not supporting his plans to seek reelection. The primary for the next election is one month away.

You have been working in manpower for the past three years and have developed considerable expertise in the area. You have also developed a commitment to stated manpower goals and have sought the achievement of those goals with considerable energy and some success. You are determined to continue the trend of success.

Your staff consists of the following persons:

Planner: Ted Jacob
Assistant planner: Betty Bloom
Program liaison officer: John Johnson
Administrative assistant: Sally Forner
Secretary: Barbara O'Shea
Director of evaluation and public relations: Fred Jones
Labor market analyst: Jane Farrell

Although these persons have distinctive titles, you have arranged work assignments so that all employees are involved in all types of ongoing activities. It is important to note that Barbara is a very good secretary and is quite capable of carrying out tasks that require personal tact and political finesse when she is instructed to do so. She is not one to undertake such tasks without specific instructions, however.

You personally have undertaken to develop and utilize a strong advisory council capable of making significant contributions to program success; your main problem with the council is that Charlie Barr, director of Brownsville's Office of Education, an operator of programs funded under CETA, succeeded in getting himself appointed chairman at the first meeting and still retains that post.

You have been out of your office for a week at a most inconvenient time. You were one of several staff directors called to Washington to participate in an Employment and Training Administration planning conference and to appear before the House Subcommittee on Elementary, Secondary, and Vocational Education, which is trying to work out a better means of integrating VocEd and CETA efforts. You left town on Monday, February 10. At that time, your staff was putting the finishing touches on an evaluation of ongoing programs which your staff had carried out in conjunction with the members of the advisory council. You are excited about both the success of this council training effort, which saw previously disinterested council members take an active role and gain a much better understanding of manpower, and its product, a very thorough and honest accounting of the status of current programs. For the first time the members of the advisory council who are not personnel professionals are excited about the chance to apply their knowledge and some rational efficiency criteria to the allocation of available program funds. You returned to town on Saturday, February 15, and because Monday, February 17, was a holiday, you went directly to join your family at your weekend home. You have heard nothing from your office since you left town.

172

EXERCISE 15 Problems in Administration of Employment and Training Programs: An In-Basket Exercise

Now it is Tuesday, February 18. You arrive at the office at 8:10 and go directly into your office. You anticipate a very busy week because you think the advisory council is scheduled to meet on February 26 to draw up its recommendations for the allocation of funds to program operators for the coming fiscal year. The council will review all program proposals and prioritize them, indicating the order in which programs should be funded once Congressional appropriation of funds is completed. You anticipate trouble from the local educational establishment because the evaluation of several VocEd and Adult Basic Education programs receiving CETA funds was very negative and advisory council members are suggesting funding alternative program operators. You had left Ted Jacob in charge of the office because he is your chief assistant within the formal structure of the organization, and because you wanted to test his administrative skills under what promised to be rather difficult conditions. You had asked him to have the completed evaluation and program proposal document on your desk and ready for printing by 8:00 this morning. Not finding the document, you turn to your in-basket and proceed to read its contents, and to consider the list of things to do you brought from Washington.

			FEBRUARY			
S	M	T	W	T	F	S
						1
2	3	4	5	6	7	8
9	10	11	12	13	14	15
16	17	18	19	20	21	22
23	24	25	26	27	28	

Document Responses

Answer the following questions about each of the documents on the following pages: Place your responses on the page with the document. Use additional paper, if necessary.

1. What action is called for?

2. How urgent is it?

3. When will you carry it out (in relation to the other tasks that must be done)?

4. What are the political implications of the decision you must make? (Note: "Politics" in this question includes intraoffice politics involving the personalities of your staff members as well as inter-agency, city, and other politics.)

5. What conflict, if any, does the document present between your short-term interest and expediency and your long-term interests?

TO __Bob__

DATE __2/18__ TIME __8:05__

WHILE YOU WERE OUT

__Ted's wife__ CALLED

OF _____

PHONE _____

TELEPHONED	✓	IN PERSON TO SEE YOU	
PLEASE CALL		WANTS TO SEE YOU	
WILL CALL AGAIN		RETURNED YOUR CALL	

MESSAGE __Ted is sick, will not be able to come to work today.__

TAKEN BY __Barb__

175

TO **Bob**

DATE **2/18**   TIME **8:01**

WHILE YOU WERE OUT

Mark Allen CALLED

OF **mayor's office**

PHONE _____

TELEPHONED		IN PERSON TO SEE YOU	
PLEASE CALL	✓	WANTS TO SEE YOU	
WILL CALL AGAIN		RETURNED YOUR CALL	

MESSAGE **please call as soon as possible**

TAKEN BY **Barb**

CITY OF BROWNSVILLE
MANPOWER PLANNING OFFICE
INTRAOFFICE MEMO

TO: Bob   **DATE**: February 14, 19--
FROM: Ted
SUBJECT: Daily Report

Happy Valentine's Day!

The printer did not get the job done at noon, but I've agreed that we'll pay the necessary overtime in order to get it into the evening mail so it can be delivered tomorrow. Sally will scream, but I didn't see any alternative.

I told the printer that we will pick up the remaining copies Tuesday morning, so that we don't have to wait for their delivery.

It will be very good to have you back in charge. I'm worked out!

CITY OF BROWNSVILLE
MANPOWER PLANNING OFFICE
INTRAOFFICE MEMO

TO: Bob   **DATE:** Feb. 14, 19--

FROM: Barbara

SUBJECT: Mayor's Public Employment

Mark Allen from the Mayor's office called several times while you were gone. I left messages for Ted to return the calls, but Allen keeps calling. Allen said that the Mayor needs more Title VI positions right away and that he hopes the council will prioritize accordingly on Wed. night.

CITY OF BROWNSVILLE
MANPOWER PLANNING OFFICE
INTRAOFFICE MEMO

TO: Bob   **DATE:** Feb. 14, 19--

FROM: Barbara

SUBJECT: Advisory Council Meeting

Barr sent over a copy of the required public notice about the advisory council meeting. Barr said he is having the notice posted in all required places and that notice has been sent to <u>The News</u>. I'll attach a copy of the notice below.

NOTICE OF PUBLIC MEETING
OF
BROWNSVILLE MANPOWER PLANNING ADVISORY COUNCIL

DATE: February 19, 19--

TIME: 7:30 p.m.

PLACE: Washington School Auditorium

notice required by B.O. 57-637J

CITY OF BROWNSVILLE

OFFICE OF THE MAYOR

MEMORANDUM

TO: Max   **DATE**: February 13, 19--

FROM: Nile

SUBJECT: Urgent!

What are you trying to do to me? Suddenly I have calls
coming in from Shine, from six state legislators, and from
practically everyone who works for the education system re-
minding me what a good job VocEd and Adult Basic Education
have been doing, stressing the importance of continuing and
increasing their funding, and expressing fears that you guys
are out to destroy "these valuable programs." Have you forgotten that the primary is next month? We don't need this
kind of heat. See me ASAP.

CITY OF BROWNSVILLE
MANPOWER PLANNING OFFICE
INTRAOFFICE MEMO

TO: Bob   **DATE**:

FROM: Betty

SUBJECT: Promotion

I understand that there is a possibility that Ted will soon be demoted or dismissed. I would like to point out that I have been working in this office since its first day of operation and that I have the necessary qualifications and experience for his job. Thus I would like to state my desire to be considered for the job of Planner when it becomes available.

UNITED STATES SENATE

Office of Senator Fred Burris

February 10, 19--

Mr. Robert Max
Manpower Planning Office
City Hall
Brownsville

Dear Mr. Max:

Although I am not a Senator from your fine State, I have served for many years on the Senate's Committee on Interior and Insular Affairs and its Subcommittee on Indian Affairs and have become familiar with the activities of your local Native American Services Association. Very few organizations have achieved as fine a record of service to Native Americans as this one.

One of my staff aides has brought to my attention a manpower program proposal drawn up by the Association. It is an exciting plan, one that promises significant contribution to a segement of the Native American population, and it needs an experimental year of operation at once. Thus I heartily encourage you to facilitate the funding of their proposed program with CETA funds available to your prime sponsor area. I look forward to hearing good things from your area in the near future.

Sincerely,

Fred Burris
U.S. Senator

182

JOB ACTION, INC.

BROWNSVILLE

February 12, 19--

Mr. Robert Max
Manpower Planning Office
City Hall
Brownsville

Dear Bob,

What is happening here, anyway? Charlie Barr's secretary called yesterday with the message that the advisory council meeting has been rescheduled for February 19. I have been hoping to get several of us from the board together before this next meeting to map out a strategy to keep Charlie from railroading through funds for VocEd and Adult Basic Ed at the next meeting, but was holding off until we all received copies of the evaluation document. I would particularly like to get together with the nonpractitioner members of the board who have participated in the evaluation. Charlie may or may not have anticipated such a move, but he has certainly made the task of opposing him much more difficult.

At any rate, would you please try to schedule a meeting to include the nonpractitioners and the members of the board from the O.I.C., the Employment Center, NYC, Indian Power, AFL-CIO, and any others whom you feel would be interested and cooperative.

Thanks for your help in this important matter.

Sincerely,

Jean Cooper

CITY OF BROWNSVILLE
MANPOWER PLANNING OFFICE
INTRAOFFICE MEMO

TO: Bob   **DATE:** February 14, 19--

FROM: Fred

SUBJECT: Vacation

After all the work getting the plan and evaluation together, I need a vacation. I'd like to leave for Denver on Thursday, Feb. 20. I plan to take seven days' vacation and will return to work on Monday, March 3.

CITY OF BROWNSVILLE
MANPOWER PLANNING OFFICE
INTRAOFFICE MEMO

TO: Bob   **DATE:** February 13, 19--

FROM: Ted

SUBJECT: Daily Report

This place was a madhouse today--everyone very harried and grouchy. But we did it! All parts of the evaluation and plan were in my hands by noon except for John's. He did a lot of loud complaining but finally got his section in at 1:30. We got it all organized and to the printer at 3:30. The printer has agreed to get it done by noon tomorrow and to mail copies to all members of the council, so they should get them on Saturday. That doesn't give them the week's study time they mandated, but given the circumstances I think the staff has done an admirable job.

I let everyone go home early today as a reward for the job well done. Perhaps that will blunt the demands for extra pay, etc.

The final document evaluated the on-going programs as follows:

Outstanding
   Up, Up, and Away
   Neighborhood Youth Corps

Good
   Brownsville Employment Center
   Job Action, Inc.
   Brownsville O.I.C.
   Oakridge Community Action Program

Satisfactory
   Jobs for Everyone
   AFL-CIO Opportunities Program
   Indian Power

Poor
   VocEd
   Adult Basic Education

I'm sorry you weren't here to make any necessary adjustments.

CITY OF BROWNSVILLE
MANPOWER PLANNING OFFICE

TO: Norman Nile, Mayor   DATE:

Bob —
This requires your signature.
Barb

FROM: Robert Max, Director

SUBJECT: Summary of Evaluation Report

Our completed evaluation report on ongoing manpower programs is now in the hands of all advisory council members, wh
who participated in the evaluation. The document will be
summarized and hopefully will serve as a basis for discussion
at the advisory council meeting of February 19, which will
adopt recommendations for next year's plan.

The evaluation looks at several aspects of all programs, including placement success, client evaluation of program, cost
per client, fiscal management, and completion rate, and con-
cludes with an overall classification of the programs as follows:

Outstanding
    Up, Up, and Away
    Neighborhood Youth Corps

Good
    Brownsville Employment Center
    Job Action, Inc.
    Brownsville O.I.C.
    Oakridge Community Action Program

Satisfactory
    Jobs for Everyone
    AFL-CIO Opportunities Program
    Indian Power

Poor
    VocEd
    Adult Basic Education

CITY OF BROWNSVILLE
MANPOWER PLANNING OFFICE
INTRAOFFICE MEMO

TO: Bob   DATE: 2/13

FROM: John

SUBJECT: Personal affairs at the office

That student intern you brought in here is really something else. He seems to spend all of his time making eyes at Jane and following her around. I never see him do any work. It's not so bad if he doesn't work, but he is also interfering with Jane's work and I think you should ask him to get to work or else to get out so that the rest of us can do our jobs.

UNITED STATES HOUSE OF REPRESENTATIVES

**Office of John Shine
Central District**

Mr. Robert Max, Director   February 10, 19--
Manpower Planning Office
City of Brownsville

Dear Bob,

  Mr. Charlie Barr, Director of the Brownsville Office of
Education, has just provided me with a long report on the
many accomplishments of his agency in carrying out its responsibilities under the Comprehensive Employment and Training Act (CETA). I have just completed a public letter of
commendation to Mr. Barr and forwarded a copy to the editor
of The News.

  I am writing to commend your office for funding Mr. Barr's
operations so generously in the past and to stress the importance of your continuing to do so in the future. As you know,
several other Representatives in Congress have joined me in
a study of the value of formula grants such as that which
supports your activities. It is through your continued support for projects such as Mr. Barr's that you can assure the
continuation and possible expansion of such decentralized
control over federal funds.

                                        Sincerely,

                                        John Shine

CITY OF BROWNSVILLE
MANPOWER PLANNING OFFICE
INTRAOFFICE MEMO

TO: Bob   **DATE:** Feb. 13, 19--

FROM: Barbara

SUBJECT: Program Clients

Two participants in the Jobs for Everyone program came to
the office today to see you. They said you invited anyone
with a problem regarding their program to come and talk with
you when you spoke to the whole group last month. They said
the matter is urgent, involving misuse of program funds and
discrimination against some clients. I have their names and
phone numbers on file.

CITY OF BROWNSVILLE
MANPOWER PLANNING OFFICE
INTRAOFFICE MEMO

TO: Bob   **DATE:** February 13, 19--

FROM: Ted

SUBJECT: Public Employment positions for the Mayor

   The mayor's office is after more Public Employment (PE) positions and is asking us to have the council allocate some to his office at next week's meeting I have told Mark Allen that PE is not on the agenda for this month's meeting --that a committee is still working on the prioritization-- but he keeps calling back and obviously wants to pressure you. As you know, the mayor's office operates as a campaign headquarters during campaigns, and PE positions will simply allow regular City Hall workers to spend more time on the campaign. We could get into real trouble with E.T.A. for making that kind of placement.

190

The Mayor   February 6, 19--
City Hall
Brownsville

Your Honor,

   As an American citizen I strongly object to the use of my
hard-earned money, taken away in taxes, to support immoral
welfare chiselers. I work hard for my money, and my family
cannot afford any luxuries in these days of rampant inflation.
It makes me sick to see these welfare bums getting paid for
enrolling in your so-called manpower program and then sitting
around the Skills Training Center all day, smoking and drinking. They never do any work but they collect good money.

   I have many friends who feel the same way, and we all want
you to know that we won't vote for you unless you stop throw-
ing away our tax money on these bums.

                                          Sincerely,

                                          Cyrus Beaten

Bob -
PLEASE HANDLE THIS
    Norm

191

CITY OF BROWNSVILLE
MANPOWER PLANNING OFFICE
INTRAOFFICE MEMO

TO: Bob   **DATE:** Feb. 13, 19--

FROM: John

SUBJECT: Ted

While you have been gone, Ted has been acting in a most unprofessional manner. He has come to work late every day. At the same time he has demanded that we do an incredible amount of work requiring several extra hours. It is not fair for the rest of us to have to work under a man with so little dedication to the job who demands that everyone work overtime for no pay.

192

CITY OF BROWNSVILLE
MANPOWER PLANNING OFFICE
INTRAOFFICE MEMO

TO: Bob   DATE: Feb. 12, 19--

FROM: Ted

SUBJECT: Daily Report

I told everyone this morning that they would have to have their sections of the evaluation and program proposal document on my desk by noon tomorrow so that we can get it to the printer by 4 p.m. The printer has agreed to do it on a rush basis and thinks he can have it ready Friday noon. Don't know how we'll ever get it distributed, but it can't possibly be done any sooner.

Several staff members claim that they will have to work all night tonight to get done and want some reimbursement, or at least a meal allowance. Sally keeps saying it's impossible. I've got everyone to agree to hold off on the matter until you get back.

CITY OF BROWNSVILLE
MANPOWER PLANNING OFFICE
INTRAOFFICE MEMO

TO: Bob   **DATE:** Feb. 12, 19--

FROM: Fred

SUBJECT: The News

We have a big problem. Gary Schaller from The News called. The paper has received a public letter of commendation from Congressman Shine praising the accomplishments of Charlie Barr and the Office of Education's CETA programs. Somehow Schaller found out that we evaluated Barr's program as the worst of our current programs. The News plans to print a story on the discrepancy next to Shine's letter, possibly on page 1. Schaller said they planned to do the story on Sunday, Feb. 16, but I talked him into holding back and talking with you because you might bring some clarifying information back from D.C. with you. He expects to see you Tuesday morning.

194

BROWNSVILLE COMMISSION ON MINORITIES

MEMORANDUM

TO: Robert Max
      Manpower Planning Office

DATE: February 10, 19--

FROM: James Wood
        Director

SUBJECT: Discontinuation of CETA Funding of VocEd Programs

Several clients of VocEd programs have come to us with complaints of racial slurs and evidence of discrimination in the selection of clients of the programs. We find these problems especially alarming when perpetrated by a government agency operating on tax revenues. We are pleased that your office has had the courage to complete a negative evaluation of the VocEd programs and share your concern about avoiding a public discussion of the agency's record of discrimination.
But we also feel that it is important that the negative evaluation be examined at the next council meeting and result in a discontinuation of VocEd use of manpower funds. We shall be present to make sure that all necessary barriers to the continued use of manpower funds by VocEd will be raised, and would welcome prior discussion of tactics with you.

CITY OF BROWNSVILLE
MANPOWER PLANNING OFFICE
INTRAOFFICE MEMO

TO: Bob   **DATE**: Feb. 12, 19--

FROM: Barbara

SUBJECT: Stationery

We're down to our last box of letterhead and Sally says we can't order any more. Please arrange something with her PRONTO! We'll run out within a month, and orders require three weeks for delivery.

CITY OF BROWNSVILLE
MANPOWER PLANNING OFFICE
INTRAOFFICE MEMO

TO: Bob   **DATE:** February 11, 19--

FROM: Ted

SUBJECT: Daily Report

You'll not be surprised to learn that Charlie Barr has tried to push us to the wall again. He called this morning to say that he was advancing the date of the advisory council meeting from Feb. 26 to Feb. 19 because of the need to obtain final approval of the plan as quickly as possible to enable program operators to gear up for next year's programs with maximum lead time. However, I'm sure he knows you will be out of town for the week, and he also knows that we are still putting the finishing touches on the evaluation and plan proposal document. I'm sure he is trying to limit the ability of his competitors to mobilize opposition and limit his hold on CETA funds.

This means that after you get back you'll have only $1\frac{1}{2}$ days at the office before the meeting. I tried to get Barr to change his mind and leave the meeting as scheduled but he was determined and said he was notifying all council members.

197

CITY OF BROWNSVILLE
MANPOWER PLANNING OFFICE
INTRAOFFICE MEMO

TO: Bob   DATE: 2/11
FROM: Jane
SUBJECT:

I got another parking ticket while on official business. I've already had five this year and that's the limit, so I need you to call the mayor's office and get it fixed. I've got the ticket in my desk when you can get to it. The hearing is scheduled for Feb. 21.

Thanks Bob!

CITY OF BROWNSVILLE
MANPOWER PLANNING OFFICE
INTRAOFFICE MEMO

TO: Bob   **DATE:** Feb. 10, 19--

FROM: Sally

SUBJECT: Budget

We cannot continue our current level of operating expenses and stay below the 20% maximum that CETA places on administrative expenses. Do you want me to start revising our accounting methods, or do you have a plan for cutting expenses?

CITY OF BROWNSVILLE
MANPOWER PLANNING OFFICE
INTRAOFFICE MEMO

TO: Bob   **DATE:** February 10, 19--

FROM: Ted

SUBJECT: Daily Report

Because you'll be gone all week and I want to report all of importance to you when you get back, I'm going to write a daily memo of what's happened so that I don't forget anything.

Sally told me we urgently need to find more operating funds, that we won't be able to pay staff salaries by May if we don't do something. I told her to write you a memo for immediate action when you get back.

The evaluation and plan proposal document is coming along. We should have it distributed by the middle of next week, which will give everyone a week to study it before the next advisory council meeting.

Nothing else significant at the office today. You'll be interested to know that as I left the airport this morning I saw Charlie Barr getting off a plane arriving from D.C. --wonder what he was doing there!

February 8, 19--

Dear Bob,

I have thoroughly enjoyed participating in the evaluation
of ongoing programs. During my first $2\frac{1}{2}$ years as a citizen member of the advisory council I felt I was a complete
outsider of little or no value, without sufficient knowledge to make a significant contribution. Participating in
the evaluation has really turned me on to the job and I
look forward to an extended discussion of the various program proposals in light of our evaluations at the next
council meeting. I plan to push for the denial of more money to those programs which have poor evaluations.

Sincerely,

Chuck Daniels

PROFESSIONAL PLANNERS SOCIETY

February 3, 19--

Mr. Robert Max
Manpower Planning Office
City Hall
Brownsville

Dear Mr. Max:

Mr. Ted Jacob, the Planner in your office, has been nom-
inated for a position on the Directorate of our organization. Members of the Directorate are elected and, in order
to familiarize all members of the Society with the various
candidates for Society office, we publish a booklet intro-
ducing all candidates. We would greatly appreciate your
providing us with a descriptive evaluation of Mr. Jacob's
capabilities, both as a planner and in the field of management (the Directorate is responsible for the management of
our Society). I realize that we are very late in making
this request, but we need your statement not later than
February 20 in order to insure sufficient time for printing
and distribution before the election.

Thanking you in advance for your help.

Sincerely,

James Ergo

James Ergo
Elections Chairman

NATIVE AMERICAN SERVICES ASSOCIATION

February 7, 19--

Mr. Robert Max
Manpower Planning Office
City Hall
Brownsville

Dear Bob:

As you know, we submitted a proposal to be funded as operators of a vocational training program under last year's
CETA appropriations, but the advisory council decided that
our proposal and the proposal submitted by the VocEd people
offered essentially the same services and the available
program funds were given to them, not us. It occurs to me
that it is that time of year again, and our organization
would like to apply for CETA funding once again. I don't
need to point out that we have closer ties with the local
Indians than any other potential program operators because
of our extensive involvement in many Indian programs or that
Indians now comprise more than 15% of the area's unemployed.

We have spent a great deal of time over the past several
months developing an exciting and innovative program that
will succeed in integrating large numbers of Native Americans into the local labor force on a permanent basis. We
would greatly appreciate it if you will give us timely notice to submit our proposal so that it can receive full consideration during the planning cycle for the next program
year.

We appreciate your help and consideration.

Sincerely,

John Lightfoot

John Lightfoot

203

CITY OF BROWNSVILLE
MANPOWER PLANNING OFFICE
INTRAOFFICE MEMO

TO: Bob   **DATE:** Feb. 10, 19--

FROM: Jane

SUBJECT: Stan Hatch

I'd like to go on record with a very positive evaluation of the work Stan Hatch is doing. Of all the student interns we have had in our office, he is the most competent and enthusiastic by far. In addition to his work contribution it is a pleasure to have him around. I know that you have to evaluate the interns for the university and I just wanted you to have this input for that evaluation.

Notes brought back from D.C.

To do immediately:

1. ARDM wants description of planning/evaluation Process — ASAP

2. ETA in DC wants report on functions and use of advisory council complete with comments from all council members

3. Shine's staff aide wants report on office activities

4. Tell OIC about change in Regs

5. Prepare report on Public Employment Utilization. (Doc seems concerned about patronage, etc.)

6. House Subcommittee wants report on local relations w/ Voc Ed by next week. Get Fred on this right away. Send to Al Greene.

G.   In-basket Evaluation Techniques

In-basket exercises are often used to assess potential or current administrative skills. In such situations, assessors are often asked to write a report about how an individual has done relative to the situations in the in-basket. The following is one format for such a report. It points out skill areas which can be evaluated. This in-basket exercise could be used with observers (assessors) who would write such a report about other participants' in-basket approaches (a learning experience for both the assessor—assessment being a common and important administrative task—and for those assessed). Or, this format could be used for further discussion, drawing attention to the listed administrative skills.

Assessment Report

An assessment report should include the actions taken, the content of the responses, and the manner (style) in which they were   performed. The report should indicate the following:

1. *Planning and organizing.* Did the respondent set up specific schedules such as "Thursday this week," or "before Monday;" or general, "on my return," "next week," "soon;" or indefinite, "see me next month"?

    Did the respondent: 1. Set up a priority of items? 2. Relate one item to another? 3. Make use of background information? 4. Make unwarranted assumptions? 5. Introduce fictitious elements into the situation?

2. *Decision making.* Did the subject postpone or suspend decisions? Did the subject make indefinite comments, such as "see me" or "let's discuss"? Initiate action such as making suggestions or asking for information, or make a final decision?

    In the area of delegation, did the individual delegate responsibility completely? Delegate but provide generalized guidance on direction, or direct subordinates to execute specific orders?

3. *Written communication.* Were comments clear and to the point? Were vocabulary and grammar proper?

4. *Amount of work or energy level.* Did the subject act on all the items? Outline a busy or easy schedule for the next few days? How much total material did the subject write, etc?

    An indication of other factors such as analytical ability, agressiveness, and risk taking may also be included.

206

SECTION
C

Evaluation

EXERCISE 16
Evaluation of Government Programs

Purpose

1. To experience the complexities and difficulties associated with the evaluation of public organizations and their programs.
2. To learn to identify the variety of organizational and program elements that need to be considered in such evaluations.
3. To understand the use of important tools of evaluation of public agencies: units of service output and measurable indicators of goal achievement.

Preparation

Read the introduction.

Group Size

Any size.

Time Requirement

Ninety minutes.

Physical Setting

Movable chairs if work is to be done in small groups.

Related Issues

Planning, implementation, prioritizing, and objective setting.

A. Introduction

The evaluation of public agencies and their programs is not a simple task. In fact, public administrators have only begun to identify the problems involved and have perfected only a few techniques with very limited applicability. The fundamental reason for this continuing failure in the development of the practice of public management is that the outputs of most public agencies are exceedingly difficult to specify and measure.

Measures of efficiency and effectiveness, the tools of evaluation, are much easier to specify for the activities of the private sector, which tend to be evaluated by the quantities of goods and services produced and revenues generated. The marketplace is assumed to correct for differences in the quality of competing products and even to specify what should and will be produced.

For the public sector, things are not so simple. The recipients of most public goods and services do not pay for them, at least not directly. Most of the agencies that provide those goods and services have no competitors, so direct comparisons of the quality of outputs are impossible. In many cases, the goals of public agencies and programs are not even clearly stated, so that even a broad evaluation of goal achievement is impossible. Even worse for potential administrators, some of these agencies and programs have conflicting goals, so that an evaluation must inevitably show failure to achieve one or more goals even when it indicates progress toward or achievement of others.

The root of the problem, of course, is the basing of public agency goals on decisions made in the political arena. Political decisions are usually based on compromises among different, frequently conflicting, interests. Such compromises generally avoid specifics—how many of what services will be provided to whom. Instead, an amount of money is appropriated for an activity, and a primary concern of the administrator is to spend all of it. Establishing standards of quality is left to the administrator, who has no guidelines for how to establish them. Efforts to avoid negative feedback to the political decision makers becomes a substitute for efforts to achieve quality; the satisfaction of special interests is sought in order to secure positive feedback. Indicators—or even a definition—of program quality are left unexamined.

Nevertheless, demands for evaluation increase as the costs of government rise and taxpayers demand a good return for their money. These increasing demands have resulted in efforts to measure productivity, or the amount of service of a certain quality provided for a given input. Assuming constant quality, improvements in productivity could then be measured over time. Carrying out this relatively easy comparison for a public agency involved in the provision of some service, however,

210

requires the specification of some unit of service whose production can be measured against the various inputs required for its provision. This is no simple task.

There are four types of units commonly used in the measurement of service outputs: (1) *activity* units, such as an outreach contact with a potential client or a counseling session; (2) *time* units, such as the number of days of child care provided or received; (3) *material* units, such as meals for the elderly or books for schools; and (4) *outcome* units, such as job placements from an employment program or reduced injuries from a safety program.*

In addition to comparing the productivity of a single agency or program over time or of two or more agencies or programs, it is also possible to evaluate a single agency by comparing its achievements with its goals. Management by objectives, a highly recommended process of management, allows the evaluation of the performance of individual employees by comparing work accomplished with a set of performance goals and a time table agreed to by the employee at the beginning of a specified time period. The evaluation of a social welfare agency or program, though, is much more difficult, both because of the enormous amount of information which must be obtained and processed and because of the need to compare the experiences of program clients with those of a matched control group who did not receive the services being evaluated. Without data or a control group, an evaluator can never be sure that any changes in the lives of clients can be attributed to the program being studied; they might have been caused by something in the environment.

Data indicating that the changes did not occur among a control group support arguments that the agency or program being studied brought about the observed changes. This type of evaluation involves at least five steps: (1) identification of goals; (2) specification of measurable indicators of goal achievement; (3) identification of the client group to be studied and of the control group; (4) collection of data; and (5) analysis of data, including comparison of client and control groups.

*The discussion to this point is based on Bruce L. Gates, *Social Program Administration*, a forthcoming Prentice-Hall text, (1980). Adapted by permission of Prentice-Hall, Inc., Englewood Cliffs, New Jersey. For the categories in this paragraph, Gates relied on Gary E. Bowers and Margaret R. Bowers, "The Elusive Unit of Service," *Human Services Monograph Series*, no. 1 (September 1976): 9.

B. Procedure

1. In small groups or as a single unit of all class members, define the unit of service output that you would use to evaluate the productivity of the following programs and proposals (*thirty minutes*):

    a. A local agency on aging seeks an additional $6,000 a year to provide an additional 600 contacts through its outreach service. (How would you determine the dollar value of one contact—how would you define the unit of service and its value?)

    b. A public employment program with a primary goal of producing job placements in the private sector and a secondary goal of income maintenance employs sixty-seven people annually at a cost of $600,000 and places fifteen in private sector employment. No individual is allowed to participate in the program for more than two years. The program seeks the same level of funding plus 7 percent for inflation for the coming year. (How would you define and value a unit of service?)

    c. Two different agencies each supply 5,000 meals for needy individuals over the course of a year. One spends $10,000, or $2 per meal, the other spends $7,500, or $1.50 per meal. Both request public funding for the coming year. (How would you measure their relative effectiveness—on the basis of what unit of service?)

    d. A day care center submits a proposal to provide supervised child care to children of migrant workers during the harvesting season. The proposal requests $5,000 to employ two persons and provide services to fifteen children, 8 hours a day for a total of fifty days. How much service is provided? Two persons for fifty days at 8 hours per day is 800 hours of service provided. But how much is received? Fifteen children for fifty days at 8 hours per day yields 6,000 hours of service received. But which is the appropriate unit of service: Units provided or units received?*

    e. Two crisis counseling centers submit identical proposals to provide 200 counseling sessions designed to alleviate family crises. Each proposal requests $4,000. (What would you need to know in order to compare the quality of the services to be provided

---

This and other examples used here are taken from Bruce L. Gates, *Social Program Administration*, a forthcoming Prentice-Hall text, (1980). Adapted by permission of Prentice-Hall, Inc., Englewood Cliffs, New Jersey.

by each program? How would you define the unit of service?)

f.   The state's Department of Tourism currently promotes tourist and convention trade for the state with a budget of $400,000. The agency requests $450,000 from the legislature for the next year and secures vigorous lobbying support from representatives of the tourist industry. (How would you define and value a unit of service?)

2.   In small groups or as a single unit of all class members, identify the goals and specify the measurable indicators of goal achievement which would be used to evaluate an agency charged with improving the transportation system of a city. It should be apparent that you must first break down the broad goal of "improving the transportation system" into a number of components, which might include improving the city bus service, improving road maintenance, improving street lighting, improving traffic flows. Then you will need to identify measurable indicators of achievement of each part of each component. In your deliberations, keep in mind that there are budgetary limits on your activities; you will not be able to do everything necessary or desirable. Your indicators should help administrators choose among various means to various goals. When you have completed this step, you should have an evaluative model which would enable you to measure the performance of a single agency in achieving its goals. In theory, at least, such an evaluation ought to be useful for deliberations over continuing, increasing, or decreasing the funding for that agency (*forty-five minutes*).

3.   Prepare a written evaluation of the tools of evaluation you have just been working with: (1) defining units of service output and (2) defining goals and measurable indicators of goal achievement. Submit your written evaluation to the instructor before leaving class (*fifteen minutes*).

C.   Discussion and Conclusions

1.   How does/should evaluation relate to planning and implementation? How would the use of PERT in the planning process aid subsequent evaluations?

2. Evaluation is customarily defined as the examination of success in or progress toward goal achievement. What is the significance, for evaluators of public organizations and programs, of the fact that these organizations and programs need the support of a variety of groups, both inside and outside the organizations, which have different and often conflicting expectations for the organizations which they hope to help embody in the goals of the organizations?*

3. What evaluation technique would you characterize as best for application to social welfare agencies?

D. Assessment of Learning

Think about what you have done in this exercise. Try to identify two or three major points that you have learned from this experience. What meaning do these points have for you as an individual and for you as an administrator? How might you put this learning to use outside the class?

Consider only what you have really learned. Don't try to figure out what other participants say they learned, or what you think you should have learned. If you feel you didn't learn anything, think about why. What could you have done to get more out of the exercise? How might the exercise have been structured differently to provide a better learning experience? What could be done in later exercises to help make them better learning experiences?

*This conflict was noted by James D. Thompson, *Organizations in Action* (New York: McGraw-Hill, 1967), p. 127.

E.   Selected Readings

Bowers, Gary E., and Bowers, Margaret R., "The elusive unit of service," *Human Services Monograph Series*, 1 (September 1976).

Gates, Bruce L., *Social Program Administration* (Englewood Cliffs, N.J.: Prentice-Hall) (1980).

Hatry, H.P., Winnie, R.E., and Fisk, D.M., *Practical Program Evaluation for State and Local Government Officials* (Washington, D.C.: The Urban Institute, 1973).

Starling, Grover, *Managing the Public Sector* (Homewood, Ill.: The Dorsey Press, 1977), ch. 9, "Implementation and Evaluation."

Wholey, Joseph S., Nay, Joe N., Scanlon, John W., and Schmidt, Richard E., "Evaluation: When is it really needed?" *Evaluation* (March 1977).

SECTION
D

Revenues and Expenditures and the Budgetary Process

EXERCISE 17

Omak County Employment and Training Advisory Council

Purpose

1. To develop an understanding of the group-based problems of decision making, resource allocation, intragroup and intergroup conflict, resistance to change, communication and leadership processes, and intraorganizational and interorganizational politics.
2. To experience these group-based problems.

Preparation

Read the introduction. Familiarize yourself with the exercise procedures and your assigned role. Appendix C gives an introduction to CETA.

Group Size

Fourteen or more with provision for additional participants as general public observers and prime sponsor planning staff.

Time Requirement

A minimum of two one-and-a-half hour sessions plus a half-hour discussion period.

Physical Setting

Rooms with tables or movable chairs so that a public hearing setting can be created.

Related Issues

Group processes, power and authority, organizational structure, group roles, problem solving, and decision making.

219

A. Introduction

Each fiscal year the Department of Labor allocates money to the various CETA prime sponsors to operate employment and training programs within their jurisdictions. The level of funding each prime sponsor receives is based upon a formula devised by the Department of Labor. How this funding is divided among the subagents is left to the discretion of the individual prime sponsors and their advisory councils.

In this exercise, an imaginary prime sponsor advisory council is involved in such a process. At the same time, focus is placed on several major problems in administration. There are four groups of players, each with a specific responsibility for the accomplishment of the goal of fund allocation to service the employment and training client groups. Interaction among team members and the teams is required for fulfillment of the objectives.

The setting for this exercise involves the Omak County prime sponsor, just entering its second year of operation. The first year was spent in getting programs implemented in the community, setting up reporting and monitoring systems, creating an evaluation design, and generally educating the public to its program and services. All things considered, it was a successful first year of operation. Contracted subagents were able to implement their programs smoothly and maintain a satisfactory level of performance throughout the year. Within the administrative planning staff, procedural policies were worked out as additional operational systems became necessary to meet Department of Labor regulations. Recently, a DOL assessment team from the regional offices gave the prime sponsors a satisfactory rating for its first year's performance. The coming year is expected to proceed with little or no disturbances. As the situation unfolds, there are several factors of which all participants need to be reminded:

1. Main goal of exercise is for the advisory council to select applicant proposals for funding and to determine funding levels for the approved proposals.
2. Several population sectors in the prime sponsor's jurisdiction have previously been designated as target groups toward whom this money should be directed. They are:

Vietnam veterans	disadvantaged families
youth	public assistance recipients
ex-offenders	older workers over fifty five

220

minority heads of households   handicapped persons
female heads of households   persons of limited English-
                              speaking ability

3. Strong political and community pressures exist within this prime sponsor's jurisdiction.
4. Approximately $1 million is to be allocated to Omak County from the Department of Labor for employment and training programs for the next fiscal year. However, the combined applicant proposals total more than the amount to be allotted (approximately, $1,711,000).
5. The decisions made by the Omak County Employment and Training Advisory Council are referred to the Board of County Commissioners as recommendations. Final selection of proposals and funding levels for employment and training programs rests with the commissioners. During the previous fiscal year, the advisory council's recommendations were approved in full for funding.

B. Procedure

1. Form four groups to be identified as follows by the exercise leader (*ten minutes*): *
   a. Omak County Employment and Training Advisory Council: six players.
   b. Omak County Employment and Training Administrative Planning Staff: one to five players.
   c. Representatives of the applicant agencies: six players.
   d. General public: remainder of group (class).
   Detailed descriptions and instructions for the four groups are located in section F.
2. This exercise proceeds as follows:
   a. Planning and preparation stage (*thirty minutes*):
      (1) Advisory council, planning staff, and applicant representatives study their roles and prepare for the advisory council meeting.
      (2) The members comprising the general public group will observe the other three groups after reviewing their own instructions.

---

*These roles should be assigned prior to the period of the exercise so that participants can be partially prepared ahead of time.

221

b. Planning staff presentation (*ten minutes*):
   The Omak County Employment and Training Administrative Planning Staff will make a short presentation to the advisory council.

c. Applicant presentations of proposals (*forty minutes*):
   Representatives from the applicant agencies will make "pitches" to the advisory council in hopes of securing funding. Each agency will have no more than five minutes to make its presentation. Persons from the advisory council, planning staff, and general public are free to ask questions regarding the proposals at this time.

d. Advisory council decision making (*sixty minutes*):
   The advisory council will select the proposals it feels merit funding and will determine funding levels. At this time, it may ask the Omak Employment and Training Planning Staff for recommendations.

e. Group reports (*thirty minutes*):
   (1) Group reports (*five minutes each*)
       Advisory council
       Prime sponsor
       Applicant representatives
   (2) Observers' reports (*fifteen minutes*)

f. Discussion (*thirty minutes or more*).

Note: The physical arrangement for the participant groups should resemble that given in figure 17.1.

```
          ┌─────────────────────────────┐
          │ Omak County Employment      │
          │ and Training Advisory Council│
          └─────────────────────────────┘

┌───────────────────────────────┐     ┌───────────────────────────┐
│ Omak County Prime Sponsor      │     │ Representatives of the    │
│ Administrative and Planning    │     │ Applicant Agencies        │
│ Staff                          │     │                           │
└───────────────────────────────┘     └───────────────────────────┘

          ┌─────────────────────────────┐
          │ General Public              │
          │ (Observers)                 │
          └─────────────────────────────┘
```

FIGURE 17.1   Physical arrangement of groups

D. Discussion and Conclusions

Utilizing the form for observers found in the instructions for the general public, each group of players should present a report to the class based on the topics found in the form. The observers' (general public) reports should begin the discussion period. Approximately fifteen minutes will be allotted to them. Next, each group of players will have five minutes for its reports. The class as a whole should then discuss the exercise, focus on those issues of group behavior that were most important in the accomplishment of the advisory council's overriding objective: to decide on their recommendation to the county commissioners for programs and funding for the next year.

Generally, this discussion should focus on the following issues (the group should try to determine which patterns of behavior led to success—accomplishment of objectives—for the different groups):

1. Leadership patterns
2. Understanding of and attention to primary objectives
3. Communication patterns
4. Achievement of goal(s)
5. Decision-making patterns
6. Group attitudes, behaviors

D. Assessment of Learning

Think about what you have done in this exercise. Try to identify two or three major points that you have learned from this experience. What meaning do these points have for you as an individual and for you as an administrator? How might you put this learning to use outside the class?

Consider only what you have really learned. Don't try to figure out what other participants say they learned, or what you think you should have learned. If you feel you didn't learn anything, think about why. What could you have done to get more out of the exercise? How might the exercise have been structured differently to provide a better learning experience? What could be done in later exercises to help make them better learning experiences?

E. Selected Readings

Bailes, J.C., *Management Budgeting for CETA*, Papers in Manpower Studies and Education (Corvallis: Institute for Manpower Studies, Oregon State University, 1975).

Gortner, H.F., *Administration in the Public Sector* (New York: John Wiley and Sons, 1977).

Nigro, F.A., and Nigro, L.G., *Modern Public Administration* (New York: Harper and Row, 1977).

Starling, G., *Managing the Public Sector* (Homewood Ill.: The Dorsey Press, 1977).

F. Participant Roles

Read the general instructions for the group to which you are assigned and the description for the role you are to perform. Do not read the other role descriptions.

Omak County Employment and Training Advisory Council

As members of this group, you are responsible for making final recommendations to the Board of County Commissioners on which proposals should be funded and at what level of funding. Last year the commissioners agreed to accept the council's funding recommendations without change.

The members of this council were appointed by the Board of County Commissioners, and they have worked hard. During the past year, they met monthly with the planning staff and succeeded in formulating directives for the planning process. The success of the first year was due largely to their administrative decision-making capabilities.

Essentially, there are two groups of members on the advisory council: three voting members and three nonvoting members. The voting members are responsible for deciding which proposals will be funded, although they have used extensive input from the nonvoting members.

Except for not being allowed to participate in the voting process, the nonvoting members have the same responsibilities as the first group. In past meetings, they have contributed extensively and often loudly. Although it was not intentional, all members of minority heritage ended up in this group. This has led to much dissension in the advisory council.

Hubert R. Jackson, voting status. You are president of one of the largest construction unions in Omak Valley. You know employment and training programs and their advantages and disadvantages in providing labor, particularly to the construction industry. Since being appointed to this council you have had a strong influence on its decisions. You support the minority contractors and the union role in the Jobs Optional Program.

224

Gladys Knowland, voting status. You are a professor of sociology at one of the private universities in Omak County. Since coming onto the council you have been educating yourself about CETA programs. In a short time, you have become the most knowledgeable about CETA matters of all the council members. It was through your efforts that several university seniors in sociology were placed with the county prime sponsor to fulfill their internship-with-public-agencies requirement for graduation. You support the Indian Services Training programs, but recognize there are serious questions being raised about mismanagement of those programs.

Louis B. Samuels, voting status. As part-time mayor of one of the rural towns in Omak County, you were concerned about the lack of job services that existed in rural Omak County. The Omak Employment and Training Office was the first agency that took direct action toward solving this problem. It placed several employment security job-search programs throughout the county. Your town was one in which these services were placed, and it has proved to be very successful. Many residents have been able to find work in the area because of this CETA service. You hope this will continue through the next fiscal year. Therefore, you strongly support the state's employment service's bid for funds. You are also the current chairman of the advisory council and are expected to provide the agenda for this meeting and act as meeting moderator.

Angela Martinez, nonvoting status. You are a homemaker volunteering your time and services to the local Latino League in Omak County. You are relatively new to the council and have in the past played a low-key role on the council. You are interested in seeing more job services being directed toward the Spanish-speaking people. Quiet, you are nonetheless aware of the nonvoting members' status on this council. Generally, you tend to want to have as much information as possible prior to the council's making a decision.

Gregory L. Chin, nonvoting status. Since coming to Omak County as a VISTA volunteer, you have been educating the community to the needs of the Asian community. Your name and work are known and supported by most of the agencies and minority organizations in Omak County. Periodically you submit articles that are printed in the local newspaper. Recently, a large number of aliens who speak very little English have come to Omak County for settlement, and the Asian-American Alliance has submitted a proposal for funding a program which addresses this target group's needs. You have been looking forward to this meeting, recognizing its importance for funding of the alliance proposal. You are concerned that the traditional CETA and employment security approaches do not seem to aid the Asian community.

Omak County Prime Sponsor Administrative and Planning Staff
For members of this group, the advisory council meeting is essential, because your entire planning for the next year will be dependent on the decisions made during

these meetings. The staff has been credited for putting new and innovative employment and training programs into operation and you are anxious to see this continue.

You are familiar with all the applicant proposals and their agencies and know that some are more clearly employment and training programs than others. Some of the programs, in particular the Indian Services Training Program, have had administrative problems during the last year. You also know that some of the non-voting members on the council are directors of agencies that are submitting proposals for funding to this council. And you are aware that they have political influence with the Board of County Commissioners. Thus, more likely than not, they will have their programs funded. Several other proposals are from agencies that have strong community interest groups backing them. If they are not funded, these interest groups can bring adverse publicity against the prime sponsor and its employment and training programs.

At this meeting, your group is expected to make a short presentation to the advisory council, briefing them on what CETA is all about, reviewing the present economic and labor situation for Omak County, and looking over last year's performance. You should also be prepared to give staff recommendations on the various proposals when asked by the advisory council.

The staff is made up of one to five persons who work very effectively together. During the past year, there were very few disagreements due to personality or attitude conflicts.

Roger Whiteman, Omak County prime sponsor director. You are a yound administrator in your mid-thirties. You hold a B.A. from a small but prestigious private college in economics and a master's in public administration from one of the top ten universities in the nation. You have ten years' experience working for employment security as a labor market analyst prior to becoming director for the Omak Valley Employment and Training programs. You and your wife and your two grade-school age daughters recently moved into a new home on Morena Lake. Thus far, you have managed to remain in good standing with the county commissioners. You like your job and are proud of your accomplishments. You plan to spend the next few years bringing to fruition the programs you have been able to get started in the first year.

Other Prime Sponsor Staff. The rest of the staff will help prepare the presentation to the advisory council. Collectively, you appreciate that you have worked well with each other and with the advisory council. You realize there have been a few problem areas in your programs during the first year, but feel justifiably proud that you have been innovative and successful beyond your early expectations. To prepare your recommendations for the council, you have divided the responsibilities for being familiar with the different applicant proposals. It would be best (for political reasons) that a member of the staff—rather than the director—make the presentation to the council. The director, however, should present the staff recommendations, when asked.

226

Representatives of Applicant Agencies. As members of this group, you have more freedom to use your own imagination and perhaps acting and debating ability than the other three groups. Once identified, each member is to select a proposal for which he or she will be an advocate. While studying your proposal, be thinking of methods to "sell" your proposal to the advisory council. Each representative will have approximately five minutes for his or her presentation to the advisory council. Be prepared to answer questions from anyone about your proposal. The complete proposal packages follow.

PROJECT OETEGA

Opportunities in Employment and Training
through English for a Growing America

(Counseling and Referral Program)

Presented by: Asian American Alliance
                              Director: Ms. Geri Bauer

Project Duration: July 1, 1979 to June 30, 1980

Amount Applied for: $127,817

The Asian American Alliance proposes to establish a class-room training program for persons of limited English-speaking ability in addition to providing basic services to the disadvantaged, unemployed, and underemployed.

General goals and related specific objectives designed to meet the outlined needs of the target group are as follows:

A. To create a comprehensive employment and training project that will lead to enhancement of career development opportunities and to suitable employment opportunities for 120 persons of limited English-speaking ability.

   1. Equip and staff a multilingual center servicing persons of limited English-speaking ability.
   2. Identify a minimum of 120 eligible applicants.
   3. Provide intake, counseling, and referral into an appropriate training activity for 120 persons.
   4. Publicize the availability of local area job opportunities in at least three languages.
   5. Place a minimum of 30 to 40 persons into classroom training.
   6. Place 30 to 40 persons into vocational training, on-the-job training, public service careers, or private employment.

B. To implement a comprehensive classroom training program designed to lead to suitable employment.

   1. Provide intensive instruction in English as a second
      language.
   2. Provide relevant adult basic education in American
      social, economic, and political systems.
   3. Provide prevocational training and exposure, including
      field trips, job applications, interviews.

   The Asian American Alliance will be seeking funds from
the Omak County prime sponsor for Project OETEGA.

Budget:

Administration	$ 3,969
Allowances	59,600
Training	45,400
Services	25,900
Total	$134,869

Analytical Data: Administration cost is 3 percent of total;
cost per positive termination: $1,124 each.

COMPREHENSIVE EMPLOYMENT AND TRAINING OPPORTUNITIES PROGRAM

(Job Placement, Career Counseling, Institutional Training)

Presented by: Pacifica State Employment
                                  Security Department

Project Duration: July 1, 1979 to June 30, 1980

Amount Applied for: $905,852

"A program to provide a comprehensive range of job
placement and career training opportunities for unemployed,
underemployed, and economically disadvantaged residents of
Omak County."

Essentially this program is designed to continue the
same services as those in the present operation. The four
CETA service delivery offices of the Employment Security
Department and the four rural stations of the Community
Action Agency in rural Omak County will continue. Job
referral and placement, counseling and testing, development
of individual and group institutional training and pre-
training and posttraining support services will be offered.

Positive terminations are estimated at 512 CETA clients.

Significant budget increases result from the following
anticipated changes:

1. Current program operating for only nine months; the
   proposed program for a full year.
2. A new salary schedule for state employees establishes
   increased cost of each position.
3. New proposal includes transfer of some public employment positions to employment and training contract;
   also some additional posts beyond those transferred
   positions.
4. Trainee allowances, the major single item ($539,720)
   constitutes 60 percent of the total budget; provides
   for twice the trainees of current year.

230

Budget:

    Funding needed for new program year $873,852
    Anticipated carryover from current
      program year   83,000

    Total $956,852

    Costs:

Administration	$ 56,661	
Allowances	539,720	
Training	38,566	
Services	195,057	
Anticipated total through June 30, 1980	$897,850	

    Carryover, funds required for
    allowances of program participants
    after July 1, 1980 $129,320

Analytical Data: Administrative cost: 6.5 percent; cost per
positive termination: $1,553 each.

MINORITY CONTRACTORS CRAFTSMEN TRAINING PROGRAM

Presented by: Minority Contractors

Project Duration: July 1, 1979, to June 30, 1980

Amount Applied for: $166,344.98

The Association of Minority Contractors indicates that contractors' organizations can do much to increase the number of participants in crafts throughout the industry by on-the-job training program in the Omak County area.

These training activities are designed to lead the applicant through phases of craftsmanship designed for a specific craft. There will be forty trainees participating during the contract period.

The training program will provide professional, technical, and crafts training to potential construction workers in the following skills: (a) electrical, (b) cement mason, (c) brick mason, (d) drywall, (e) plumbing, (f) carpentry, (g) painting, (h) equipment operators, (i) tile and carpet layers, and (j) dumptruck drivers.

The trainees will receive extensive training in a particular job classification. This will be done with thirty-four hours of actual on-the-job training and six hours of classroom instruction. Classroom orientation will be given on the proper usage of the tools for each individual craft. Classroom orientation will be provided before any trainee is assigned to a specific job.

The potential trainees will also be oriented on construction procedures in the particular craft. They have the assurance of journeymen status after the training, during which they will have been exposed to the full certification program and all its procedures.

Clients to be served:

a. Eighteen economically disadvantaged heads of household
b. Ten Vietnam veterans
c. Ten ex-offenders
d. Two unemployed females

The proposed program is designed to operate independently of other subcontractors; will be immediately responsible to the prime sponsor.

Major cost element is training ($450 per month paid to private contractor for the training aspect of participant's wage; total of this element is $136,700).

Budget:

Note that minority contractors have listed certain line-item costs under erroneous cost category headings; CETA staff has correctly placed these line-item costs in the following recapitulation:

Administration	$ 34,270
Allowances	7,710
Training	156,980
Total	$198,960

Analytical Data: Administration cost is 17.2 percent of total; cost per positive termination: $4,325 each.

JOBS OPTIONAL PROGRAM

UNITED BROTHERHOOD OF CARPENTERS AND JOINERS OF AMERICA
Instituted August 12, 1881

Our goal is to indenture young people into our carpenter program. We need young people in our craft as our average age is in the late forties at the present time. There is a need to get the young people in the community into a trade that will support them and their families, which will help in taking them off unemployment and welfare roles. Our goal is to reach the unemployed or the underemployed.

The contractor does not want to hire the beginning apprentice because the contractor loses money for the first six months due to no experience, craftsmen taking time from their duties to help the apprentices, and so on.

The apprentices are indentured into a four-year program and four years from the time they go to work will become journeymen.

Starting wage is $5.01 per hour plus $1.14 per hour in fringe benefits.

The only problem we have encountered occurs when there is a slack in work that temporarily keeps the contractor from hiring.

Our past performance in the Omak County area has been excellent. Under contract number 47-1-0987-333, we enrolled three apprentices and all three are still in the Carpenters Union. Under contract number 47-6-0856-555, we enrolled seven and all seven are still in the carpenter trade.

We feel that our Jobs Optional Program has been a success both for the community and all involved in achieving the above goals.

Sincerely,

Robert Bain
Apprentice Coordinator

234

A. Wages

    1. Administrator   11 x 384 = 4,224

    2. Secretary   11 x 212 = 2,332

                                          6,556

B. Fringe benefits

    1. Per diem   11 x 90   =   990

    2. Mileage   11 x 90   =   990

                                      1,980

    3. FICA

       a. Administrator   5.85% x 4,224 =   247

       b. Secretary   5.85% x 2,332 =   137

    4. Medical aid   413

    5. Federal unemployment insurance   33

    6. State employment security   196

    7. State labor and industry   26

                                      1,052

C. Training facilities   182

    1. Rent

    2. Rental of office machines

    3. Phone

    4. Office supplies

    Administration Costs   9,770

D. Subcontracting funds   65,130

   1040 hours x 2.505 per hour = $2,605.20

   Twenty-five apprentices x $2,605.20 each

   Total contract $74,900

COUNTY URBAN LEAGUE PROGRAM BUDGET

Fiscal Period 1979-1980

Administrative Funds

1. Administrative Cost

	% of Time	Salary July 1 to Oct. 15	No. of Months	Salary Oct. 16 to June 30	No. of Months	Total
a. Project director	50	625.00	3.5	587.50	8.5	$ 8,031.00
Project coordinator	25	260.41	3.5	276.00	8.5	3,258.00
Secretary	100	600.00	3.5	675.00	8.5	7,837.00
Bookkeeper	100	800.00	3.5	850.00	8.5	10,025.00
Total						$29,151.00

b. Fringe benefits: FICA, workmen's compensation, unemployment insurance, medical insurance (15%) $ 4,373.00

Total salaries and benefits $33,524.00

2. Operating Cost

a. Space: 950 sq. ft. @ 45¢ per sq. ft. $427.50 per month (includes utilities and custodial services) x 12 months $ 5,130.00

b. Office supplies: (desktop supplies, forms, checks, etc.) $125.00 per month x 12 months   1,500.00

c. Telephone and postage: base telephone rate toll cost and postage plus installation @ $200.00   2,000.00

d. Travel: 800 miles per month @ 13¢ per mile = $104.00 x 12 months   1,248.00

Total operating cost $ 9,878.00

3. Indirect Cost Recovery* (based on 5.4% of total budget)   18,934.00

Total administrative funds $62,335.00

*Indirect cost recovery is 5.4% of total budget request. This request is based upon our official and approved audit by the U.S. Department of Labor for Indirect Cost Recovery. These funds accrue to the operating agency and are assessed as a result of professional services provided in the areas of administrative supervision, program planning, develop-ment and evaluation, and accounting supervision. The League will provide, upon request, a copy of our Indirect Cost Recovery Proposal.

Program Cost

1. Staff Cost

	% of Time	Salary July 1 to Oct. 15	No. of Months	Salary Oct. 16 to June 30	No. of Months	Total
a. Project coordinator	75	781.25	3.5	828.16	8.5	$ 9,774.00
Emp. trng. spec. I	100	850.00	3.5	935.00	8.5	10,922.00
Emp. trng. spec. I	100	850.00	3.5	935.00	8.5	10,922.00
OJT offender spec.	50	450.00	3.5	467.50	8.5	5,549.00
OJT counslr/job develpr	100	850.00	3.5	935.00	8.5	10,922.00
Total						$48,089.00

b. Fringe benefits: FICA, workmen's compensation, unemployment insurance, medical coverage @ 15% $ 7,213.00 $55,302.00

c. Travel: 4,000 per month @ 13¢ = $520.00 × 12 months $ 6,240.00

d. Insurance and bonding: liability insurance to cover damage done to persons or to property other than that of sponsor 650.00

e. Fidelity bond to cover five members including board member 125.00

Total staff cost $ 7,015.00 $62,317.00

2. Staff Operating Cost

a. Media advertising (local newspaper, adv. empl. wkly, newsletter) $ 850.00

b. Printing empl. brochure, trainee handbook, recruitment brochure, etc. 800.00

c. Professional accounting services 500.00

d. Supportive services: tools, equipment, etc. 2,400.00

Total staff operating cost $ 4,550.00

Total services to clients $66,867.00

Training Cost: 160 @ $1,500.00 per trainee $240,000.00

Totals		
Administrative Funds	$ 62,336.00
Services to Clients	66,867.00
Training Cost	240,000.00
Total	$369,203.00

ON-THE-JOB-TRAINING PROGRAM

Presented by: Omak County Urban League, Inc.

Project Duration: July 1, 1979 to June 30, 1980

Amount Applied for: $369,203

In the past seven months the Urban League has operated an OJT Program based upon the successful operating mode established by the six years of on-the-job training placement by the National Urban League.

Specifically, the project goals are to place 160 persons in an on-the-job training situation in the Omak County area with emphasis on training in white- and blue-collar jobs. As is the Urban League's mission, the emphasis with clientele will be disadvantaged and minority people who are the most detrimentally affected by unemployment and underemployment in the permanent job market.

To achieve those goals the League will use its established network of employer contacts as well as develop new contacts and coordinate with the Employment Security Department intake and employer component. The League will contract with employers to hire a particular trainee for a full-time position in the employer's company. The League will reimburse the employer up to 50 percent of the employer's actual training costs for that participant trainee.

The league will provide comprehensive follow-up and counseling assistance for both the trainee and the employer. These activities include thirty-, sixty-, and ninety-day follow-up on the trainee, as well as an on-call status of the staff in order to assist in resolving conflicts between the employer and employee.

238

INDIANS SERVICE TRAINING PROGRAM

Presented by: Omak Indian Tribe

Project Duration: September 1, 1976, to
                                       August 31, 1980

Amount Applied for: $66,535.00

   To provide experience for Native Americans in the Omak
County through training, social service delivery, and program development is the objective of the Indians Service
Training Program. Completion of the training program will
lead to Civil Service positions in social service delivery
systems and/or specialized governmental training program
positions. Professional training will be provided in three
specific areas: social service delivery, statistical recording, and specific program development.

   Trainees for the program will be recruited from Native
American men and women who have previously indicated their
interest in improving the quality of life of Omak Valley
Indians. All trainees will be qualified and may enroll at
Manover State College under contracted studies for social
service delivery as a motivation for them to move into
professional capacities. In addition to qualifying Native
Americans for future career advancement within the Civil
Service System, the program will also enable trainees to
have a variety of training experiences as well.

(Note to ISTP representative: Many times last year you
requested help with the administration of your funds. You
never received any such assistance. You feel you have now
resolved your problems and have thus asked for increased
funding for next year. You assume that your recently
developed alliances on the council will help you get your
proposal approved.)

General Public

As members of the interested public, you will act as observers throughout the exercise. You should feel free to circulate among the groups as they study and discuss their instructions and information packets. You may also ask questions of the other groups throughout the exercise. Your questions should refer to the matter at hand.

You are not as knowledgeable about CETA and its regulations as the other three groups. Listen carefully to all that is being said and take notes if needed on all reports and presentations given to the advisory council. Pay particular attention to the council when it begins its selection of the applicant proposals.

During the exercise, be sure to share observations with the other members of the general public, keeping in mind that at the completion, the group will report to the class what it has observed. As there will be many actions taking place, use the following form to help organize and collect your observations.

Form for Observers

I. Leadership patterns
  A. Were there individual leaders for each group?
    1. How were they selected?
    2. Did they change during the course of the exercise?
  B. Did one leader emerge over the entire exercise? If so,
    1. How did this leader emerge?
    2. What leadership pattern did he or she conform to?
    3. Did other leaders come forth to replace him or her?
    4. What patterns did they conform to?
  C. Other observations
II. How well did members of the three groups understand their objectives in achieving the goal of determining program and fund-allocation recommendations within the given dollar constraints?
  A. Did members of the three groups clearly understand their objectives and the steps that needed to be taken to achieve the goal?
  B. Did each group consider the potential actions of the other two groups?
  C. Did they allow for actions of members within their own group?
  D. Other observations
III. Completeness information
  A. Was data and information exchanged between the groups in order to achieve the main goal?
  B. Was it clearly relayed?
  C. How well did the groups use the information?
  D. Other observations
IV. Achievement of goal
  A. Was the advisory council able to achieve its goal utilizing all the informa-

tion it received from the exercise itself? The planning staff? The representatives of the applying agencies?

   B. Other observations

V. Determination of advisory council's decisions

   A. How were the decisions arrived at?

   B. Was the decision making done quickly?

   C. Were alternative courses selected? (Did the council combine one proposal
with another in order to avoid duplication of services, serve more target
population groups, provide more services for the dollar?)

   D. Was each council member satisfied with the decisions made?

   E. Other observations

VI. Group attitudes and behaviors

   A. What types of attitudes were evident among the groups during the exercise?

   B. What types of behaviors resulted from these attitudes?

   C. Other observations

Economic and Labor Force Data for Omak County

Employment Developments

Total employment for the area declined from September 1978 through January
1979, dropping 6,300 workers over the five-month period. February reversed the
trend, and March followed with a measurable increase of 4,000 above January's low
of 135,000. Employment has followed a similar pattern of decline and rise over the
same time period for the past six years; however, the total employment figure for
March 1979 was 4,800 above the comparable figure one year ago.

On the positive side, substantial gains were registered over the year in four of
the major industry classifications. Contracts construction, wholesale and retail trade
service industries, and government each expanded by 1,000 workers or more. The
negative aspect was evident in the manufacturing industries and centered around the
logging, lumber, and wood products operations, reflecting the depressed market in
1978. Since lumber and wood products are the principle manufacturing industry in
the area, the soft market contributed appreciably to the high unemployment rate in
the area.

Although economic conditions have been far from favorable over the past
year, the employment level in Omak Valley has remained relatively stable and has
even been able to register some growth. Seasonal patterns have not changed, but
each of the past twelve months has registered a higher employment figure than that
for the corresponding month of the previous year.

Manufacturing

This area was down over the past ten months, with the logging and basic lumber
industries being hardest hit, due to rising material costs, a deteriorating market and
seasonal cutbacks. For the past two months, however, this industry classification

241

has improved because of an increase in the housing industry. Parkdale and Heberat Employment Security offices report heavy job orders for workers in the logging industry. Specific job titles included in this classification are warehouse workers, heavy equipment operators, choker setters, tree fallers, tree planters, assembly line workers.

Contract Construction

Like the manufacturing classification, the contract construction industry was depressed during the past year as a result of high interest rates, slow housing starts, seasonal cutbacks, and budget squeezes. Again resembling the manufacturing industry, contract construction has picked up primarily because of better housing starts and increased pipeline activities that peaked a month earlier. Expansion is expected to continue for this category over the next ninety days. Carpenters, plumbers, electricians, and iron and steel workers are job titles in this category.

TABLE 17.1   Ethnic Population Omak County, 1979

Type		Number	Percent
White		242,532	94.4%
Black		8,088	3.14%
Native American		1,643	.63%
Asian		3,700	1.44%
Others		937	.4%
	Total	256,900	100.0%

Minorities account for approximately 6 percent of the total population for Omak County and 4.4 percent, or 3,391, for its labor force total of 77,070.

TABLE 17.3   Population of Omak Valley by Age Group and Sex

Ages	All	Male	Female
15 and under	77,024	42,446	34,578
16–21	43,627	24,020	19,607
22–44	79,567	43,918	35,649
45–54	24,919	13,356	11,561
55–64	16,395	9,184	7,211
65 and over	15,368	8,369	6,999
Total	256,900	141,295	115,605

Wholesale and Retail Trade

This industry has shown a stable and steady growth over the past twelve months, giving a stabilizing influence to the otherwise fluctuating Omak Valley labor market. It appears that this expansion will continue through the coming months. Job titles here include warehouseworkers, produce workers, meat cutters, forklift operators, retail sales clerks, window decorators, buyers, clerical support.

Service Industries

Consistently showing steady expansion, the service industries even expanded throughout the recession of the past year. Like the wholesale and retail trade industry, this expansion is expected to continue. Essentially, areas having a substantial population require a large number of applicants of this classification. Parkdale is a town where many job orders of this sort are filled. In rural Omak Valley the service industries are at a minimum. Cooks, janitors, waitresses, domestics, and security are the types of jobs found within this classification.

Government

This classification was down during the past ten months because of school cutbacks, enrollment drops, budget restrictions, and terminations of contracts. At the local level, employment increased because of funding available from the CETA programs, but with the end of the fiscal year near, continued funding is uncertain. Presently the outlook for this category is tenuous. Jobs that fall into the classification are public administrators, case workers, teachers, clerks, accountants.

TABLE 17.4   Income of Families and Unrelated Persons in 1979 for Omak Valley

Income ($)	Number of Families
Less than 1,000	1,200
1,000 to 1,999	1,119
2,000 to 2,999	1,728
3,000 to 3,999	2,313
4,000 to 4,999	2,657
5,000 to 5,999	3,147
6,000 to 6,999	3,326
7,000 to 7,999	4,163
8,000 to 8,999	4,457
9,000 to 9,999	4,347
10,000 to 11,999	8,506
12,000 to 14,999	9,334
15,000 to 24,999	9,849
25,000 to 49,999	2,011
50,000 and over	336

TABLE 17.2   Resident Labor Force and Employment for the Omak Valley, May 1978 through April 1979 SMSA

	May 1978	June 1978	July 1978	August 1978	September 1978	October 1978	November 1978	December 1978	January 1979	February 1979	March 1979
Resident civilian labor force	155,600	159,300	158,300	157,400	158,400	152,500	153,000	155,700	153,800	149,500	153,700
Unemployment[1]	13,900	17,000	16,200	17,000	17,300	15,200	16,100	17,400	17,500	17,300	17,900
Percent of labor force	8.9	10.7	10.2	10.8	10.9	10.0	10.5	11.2	11.4	11.6	11.6
Seasonally adjusted rate	9.1	9.4	10.0	10.6	10.7	9.9	10.0	10.2	10.8	12.1	12.2
Employment	141,700	142,300	142,100	140,400	141,100	137,300	136,900	138,300	136,300	132,200	135,800

Projected unemployment rate for 1980 will be 9.2 percent, balance of Omak County, 8.6 percent.

The total number of persons in poverty was 19,117.

The "Near Poor" with incomes less than 125 percent of poverty level totaled 27,970.

The "Poor Poor" persons with incomes less than 75 percent of the poverty level numbered 12,345.

Based on information provided by the U.S. Department of Labor, Manpower Administration, Summary Manpower Indicators for Omak County; 1970 Census.

[1]Includes all jobless workers who are actively seeking employment regardless of whether or not they are receiving unemployment compensation.

EXERCISE 18

Red Balloon Day Care Centers: What Type of Budget?

Purpose

1. To understand the advantages and disadvantages of different types of budgets: the line-item budget, the performance budget, and the program budget.
2. To be aware of the pressures brought to bear on public agencies by different parties wanting those agencies to use different types of budgets.

Preparation

Read the introduction and complete steps 1 and 2 of the procedure. Students with no prior knowledge of the types of budgets under consideration will need to do additional reading in order to understand their techniques and uses.

Group Size

Minimum six, preferably twelve or more.

Physical Setting

Discussion will be facilitated if seating arrangements allow the members of each group to sit together.

Time Requirement

Ninety minutes.

245

A. Introduction*

The budgets of public agencies and of those ncies seeking public funds tend to be one or a combination of three or types: line item, performance, and program budgets. Each of the hree types is based on a different basic value: control, efficiency, d effectiveness, respectively. A number of hybrids have been dev bed recently, each seeking to incorporate two or all three of the alues as its bases. Included among these hybrids are PPBS (p ing-programming-budgeting system), ZBB (zero-based budgeting), program performance budgets. The shortcomings of each of the and of the three basic forms, are discussed by Wildavsky (1978).

The line-item budget simply lists types of ex ditures (salaries, wages, and benefits; travel; supplies and equipment) the amounts to be spent on each. The expenditures are usually list by department, branch office, or other subdivision of the agency. l lget requests in this form can be evaluated only on the basis of compa ns with expenditures in earlier years and by other agencies. The info ation thus provided is valuable for many forms of management con l, but it gives funding agencies no information on why the money sho be expended as planned or on the needs, outputs, and programs invol l.

The performance budget seeks to overcome one kness of the line-item budget—its failure to provide information ab outputs. A performance budget describes the relationships betwee he costs of program inputs and the program's output of services. theory, at least, it provides the clearest indication of a program's ficiency in terms of resource use. In practice, however, several probl affect the use of performance budgets. In exercise 16 you were intr ced to the problems associated with trying to define measures of un of service output. In addition, use of this type of budget requires at highly sophisticated financial management skills be applied to th llocation of various costs among various organizational department rograms, and offices that share the same functions. In addition, t type of budget provides decision makers in funding agencies with n nformation about how expenditures and outputs relate to needs to the achievement of organizational goals.

The program budget attempts to relate expenditure to the achievement of broad organizational goals. The budgetary pi ess begins with the specification of goals and objectives, procee to the

*The following discussion is based on chapter 8 of Bruce L. Gates, *Social Program Administration*, a forthcoming Prentice-Hall text, (1980). Adapted by permission of Prentice-Hall, Inc., Englewood Cliffs, New Jersey.

design of programs to meet those goals and objectives, and only then examines the costs and funding allocations involved. These steps are followed by an iterative process in which goals, objectives, and programs are scaled down until costs become realistic, or within the range of possible funding. This type of budget may cut across agency or departmental boundaries because the initial program planning stage seeks to define the best approach to achieving objectives regardless of organizational boundaries, and program plans may call for coordinated effort by more than one agency. Program budgets encourage program evaluation on effectiveness criteria—how well program objectives are achieved—rather than efficiency criteria. In practice, program budgeting has not worked well in the public sector for several reasons: agreement on goals and objectives is very hard to achieve; the environment in which public and social service agencies operate is highly fragmented and discourages multiorganizational planning or operations; planning for the achievement of broad social goals encourages very large budget requests and makes partial, less expensive approaches to problems much less attractive; and there are no inexpensive-to-implement or even useful methods for implementing program budgeting.

Three years ago a group of mothers organized an action group to deal with their need for day care services for their children. The action group discovered very quickly that there were a number of potential sources of funding to support child care services and formed a nonprofit corporation to seek such funds. Because of the lack of competition for the funds and in spite of their lack of management skills, they have secured funds from several sources. The corporation, Red Balloon Day Care Centers, currently receives funds from five sources and runs four day care centers in different parts of the city.

The bookkeeping and budgeting systems used by the group can best be described as chaotic. The funding levels sought in grant requests have been based on guesses about projected expenditures. Equipment and supplies have been purchased as needed by the staffs of the different centers, with bills forwarded to the bookkeeper for payment. The books have been little more than lists of bills received and paid and files of grant requests noting the amounts received. The bookkeeper has struggled valiantly to use the confusion of information for the preparation of the required monthly, quarterly, and annual reports to the funding agencies, but the result has not satisfied the auditors of those agencies. No one has accused Red Balloon of any intentional misuse of funds; all reviewers have commented on the sincere commitment to service of the staff. But those funding agencies have now made it clear that the cor-

247

poration will receive no further funding unless its funding requests are accompanied by sound, professionally prepared budgets.

The corporation's board of directors now must decide what type of budget technique to adopt. To help them make that decision, they have hired a management consultant team to review the needs of the various funding agencies, to explain the advantages and disadvantages of the various types of budgets from the point of view of the corporation, and to recommend which type the corporation should use. At the same time, the board has asked each of the funding agencies to identify the type of budget it would most like the corporation to use and to explain why it prefers that type.

The five current funding agencies and their primary concerns for budget information are:

1. The Children's Services Department (CSD) of the state, which disperses WIN funds directly to the corporation. CSD also disperses funds from numerous other federal programs. As a result, one of its primary budgetary concerns is its need to keep separate accounts for each program. Most of the federal programs it administers also involve state matching funds; the state's auditors insist that all state agencies submit program budgets for review. (WIN funds are intended to be used to assist current welfare recipients to obtain permanent employment. The program is funded with 75 percent federal and 25 percent state funds.)

2. The 4-Cs (Community Coordinated Child Care) Council, which contracts with local child care agencies to disperse federal and state funds provided to it by CSD and local matching funds. Its primary budgetary concern is to be able to respond to federal and state auditors by showing that funds have been legally expended according to the federal regulations governing use of the funds. (The funds distributed in this way are intended to provide subsidized day care services for potential Aid to Families with Dependent Children (AFDC) recipients and low-income families in order to help these families achieve or maintain economic self-sufficiency. Funding for the program is 60 percent federal, 20 percent state, and 20 percent local.)

3. The local CETA prime sponsor, which contracts for supportive services that will enable disadvantaged, underemployed, and long-term unemployed persons to obtain training or work experience that will result in permanent employment. The prime sponsor's primary budgetary concern is for its contractors to provide infor-

mation about the achievement of the employment goals of the program; the prime sponsor's staff wants to be able to tell the U.S. Department of Labor how many persons have secured permanent employment through the local CETA program. (The prime sponsor provides 100 percent of the funding for the services provided.)

4. The state's Vocational Rehabilitation Division, which contracts for the provision of day care services for the children of persons who are handicapped, who are engaged in some form of rehabilitation supported by the division, and who would not be able to engage in that rehabilitation program without the provision of the day care services. The division receives all of its funding from the federal government. Its major budgetary concern relating to the corporation is for information that relates the provision of day care to clients' participation in rehabilitation.

5. The local United Way Fund, which does not want fancy planning and budget documents and is concerned only with the sensible use of its funds (that is, the ratio between expenditures on services and administration, the percent of total expenditures used for staff benefits and "perks," the extent to which the services are provided to a broad segment of the community).

The management consultant team consists of holders of master's degrees in business administration. They are fond of elaborate budgetary techniques which serve as short- and long-term planning tools. Although they are also aware of the costs of using such tools, they continue to believe in the importance of rationality in planning. To them, being rational means designing programs that will help achieve the goals and objectives of an agency, a government, or a business.

The members of the board of directors continue to be the users of the day care services. Some of the mothers originally involved have ended their involvement because their children no longer need the services. Others, who remain committed to the idea regardless of their current need for service, have been joined by single and married parents of all backgrounds and economic situations who are committed to the provision of excellent day care services for the entire community. They recognize the need for accountability to funding sources as well as to clients and for adequate budgetary information as a basis for program planning. Therefore they regard the adoption of a new budget system that will address all of the relevant needs in the most satisfactory manner a very important task.

B. Procedure

1. The instructor will divide the class into the following groups (*five minutes*):

> Board of directors, Red Balloon Day Care Centers
> Management consultant team
> Business office staff, local United Way Fund
> Business manager and accountants, Children's Services Division
> Staff of the local 4-Cs Council
> Administrative officer and accounting staff, local CETA prime sponsor
> Business manager and accountants, Vocational Rehabilitation Division

If possible, all groups should be represented by at least two persons. If fewer than fourteen students are available, however, the Vocational Rehabilitation Division or the CETA prime sponsor can be eliminated from the exercise or any of the groups may be represented by a single person. Groups should not contain more than five students. If the class has more than thirty-five students, one or more of the agencies should be represented by more than one group so that individual work groups contain no more than five students.

2. Each group meets outside of class, assigns one of its members responsibility for keeping notes and organizing the presentation to the class, and completes the task(s) assigned to it in section F.

3. Each funding group spends five minutes explaining to the board of directors which type of budget it would like the board to use and submit to that agency and explains why it prefers that type of agency. This discussion will be facilitated if all members of each group sit together so that all of the participants are able to recognize who belongs to which group (*twenty-five minutes*).

4. The management consultant team presents its recommendation to the board and explains why it prefers the one type and rejects the other two types, referring specifically to the recommendations and arguments of the funding agencies (*fifteen minutes*).

5. A general discussion among all groups follows. The funding agencies argue against or support the recommendation of the consultant team. The board of directors seeks guidance and clarification that will facilitate its choice. The purpose of this part of the exercise is *not* to determine which group can win the most debate points; instead, the purpose is to clarify and articulate the various strengths and weaknesses of the different types of budgets. The students

should concentrate on examining all the implications of the strengths and weaknesses of each (*fifteen minutes*).

6. While the other students take a break (or work on something else), the board of directors meets to decide which type of budget the corporation will use in the future and to prepare its explanation to the other students of why it has chosen that type (*fifteen minutes*).

7. Discussion and conclusions (*twenty minutes*).

C.   Discussion and Conclusions

The board of directors announces and explains its decision. The students then leave their roles and, as a class, discuss together the merits of the board's decision and try to reach a consensus on the best way to resolve the dilemma illustrated in this exercise: the need facing public agencies to choose between alternative types of budgets. No further discussion should be necessary.

D.   Assessment of Learning

Think about what you have done in this exercise. Try to identify two or three major points that you have learned from this experience. What meaning do these points have for you as an individual and for you as an administrator? How might you put this learning to use outside the class?

Consider only what you have really learned. Don't try to figure out what other participants say they learned, or what you think you should have learned. If you feel you didn't learn anything, think about why. What could you have done to get more out of the exercise? How might the exercise have been structured differently to provide a better learning experience? What could be done in later exercises to help make them better learning experiences?

E. Selected Readings

Gates, Bruce L., *Social Program Administration* (Englewood Cliffs, N.J.: Prentice-Hall, 1980), ch. 8.

Golembiewski, Robert T., and Radin, Jack, *Public Budgeting and Finance: Readings in Theory and Practice*, 2d ed. (Itasco, Ill.: F.E. Peacock, 1975).

Gundersdorf, John, "Management and financial controls," in Wayne F. Anderson, Bernard J. Friden, and Michael J. Murphy, eds., *Managing Human Services* (Washington, D.C.: International City Management Association, 1977).

Hycle, Albert C., and Shafritz, Jay M., *Government Budgeting: Theory, Process, Politics* (Oak Park, Ill.: Moore Publishing Co., 1978).

Macleod, Roderick K., "Program budgeting works in non-profit institutions," *Harvard Business Review* 49 (September/October 1971).

Wildavsky, Aaron B., "A budget for all seasons? Why the traditional budget lasts," *Public Administration Review* 38 (November/December 1978).

F. Participant Roles

Group Tasks

Board of directors, Red Balloon Day Care Centers

Become familiar enough with the three types of budget under consideration — line item, performance, and program—to be able (1) to understand and evaluate the arguments made in support of and against your use of each, and (2) to decide which type to adopt after listening to those arguments for fifty-five minutes in class. The primary question to keep in mind at all times is which type will be most useful to your organization, given its many needs and the various demands placed on it.

Management consultant team

Read the description of the management consultant team in section A. Analyze the information and record-keeping needs of the Red Balloon agency, decide which budget system you will recommend to its board of directors, and prepare to explain to the board why the system you recommend is better than those recommended by the funding agencies. To carry out this latter task effectively you must anticipate the recommendations of those agencies. You will have fifteen minutes of class time to explain and defend your position.

Business office staff, local United Way Fund

Read the description of your primary concerns for budget information in section A. Decide which type of budget you would like Red Balloon to use when it submits funding requests and expenditure reports. Choose the type which most closely suits your needs. Then prepare a five-minute statement to be made in class to the Red Balloon board of directors indicating your choice and the reasons for your choice. Be prepared to defend and argue in favor of your choice during in-class discussion with the board of directors and the other funding agencies.

Business manager and accountants, Children's Services Division
Read the description of your primary concerns for budget information in section A. Decide which type of budget you would like Red Balloon to use when it submits funding requests and expenditure reports. Choose the type which most closely suits your needs. Then prepare a five-minute statement to be made in class to the Red Balloon board of directors indicating your choice and the reasons for your choice. Be prepared to defend and argue in favor of your choice during in-class discussion with the board of directors and the other funding agencies.

Staff of the local 4-Cs Council
Read the description of your primary concerns for budget information in section A. Decide which type of budget you would like Red Balloon to use when it submits funding requests and expenditure reports. Choose the type which most closely suits your needs. Then prepare a five-minute statement to be made in class to the Red Balloon board of directors indicating your choice and the reasons for your choice. Be prepared to defend and argue in favor of your choice during in-class discussion with the board of directors and the other funding agencies.

Administrative officer and accounting staff, local CETA Prime Sponsor
Read the description of your primary concerns for budget information in section A. Decide which type of budget you would like Red Balloon to use when it submits funding requests and expenditure reports. Choose the type which most closely suits your needs. Then prepare a five-minute statement to be made in class to the Red Balloon board of directors indicating your choice and the reasons for your choice. Be prepared to defend and argue in favor of your choice during in-class discussion with the board of directors and the other funding agencies.

Business manager and accountants, Vocational Rehabilitation Division
Read the description of your primary concerns for budget information in section A. Decide which type of budget you would like Red Balloon to use when it submits funding requests and expenditure reports. Choose the type which most closely suits your needs. Then prepare a five-minute statement to be made in class to the Red Balloon board of directors indicating your choice and the reasons for your choice. Be prepared to defend and argue in favor of your choice during in-class discussion with the board of directors and the other funding agencies.

253

SECTION
E

Public Personnel Management

EXERCISE 19

Affirmative Action at Midstate University

Purpose

1. To develop an understanding of the issues related to equal employment opportunity.
2. To develop an appreciation for the difficulties associated with accommodating conflicting constituencies involved with affirmative action programs.

Preparation

Read the introduction and step 1 of the procedure.

Group Size

Any size, broken into groups of five to seven members.

Time Requirement

Ninety minutes.

Physical Setting

Movable chairs or facilities for small groups to meet without disturbing other groups.

Related Issues

Goal setting, group values, group conflict, external relations, social responsibility, intergovernmental relations, employee relations.

A. Introduction

Since the early 1960s, and particularly since the passage of the Civil Rights Act of 1964, equal employment opportunity (EEO) and affirmative action programs for women and minorities have been given increasing attention by the public and by work organizations. This has been no less true for government organizations than for private firms. Government agencies, such as the Equal Employment Opportunity Commission, Office of Federal Contract Compliance Programs, HEW, Department of Labor, and others, have aggressively investigated organizational employment practices and encouraged public and private employers to make personnel decisions on the basis of job requirements and job qualifications, rather than on race, ethnic background, age, or sex. Private and public employers, employment agencies, and unions have been directed by the law, court cases, and enforcement agencies to use reliable (consistent) and valid job-related criteria and predictors for their employee decisions.

Even though public attitude and policy supports fuller use of women and minorities, resistance to affirmative action and EEO programs remains. This exercise provides a glimpse into some of the problems associated with these efforts.

B. Procedure

1. Prior to class, read the following case:

In the Public Service?

Jack: I've called this meeting, today, because of a problem we're facing. As you know we have been under affirmative action guidelines now for five years. Also, as you know, these guidelines are becoming more rigidly enforced. In particular, you know that we're being cited for discriminating against females in several job classifications—administration, administrative services, and office managers. Well, the secretary and I have met several times with Jeff Donnelly of the regional office of HEW; and we've come to an agreement as to what we need to do. Here's what we agreed to. From now on we cannot ask female applicants to state on the application blank their marital status, future marriage plans, the number of children they have, husband's occupation, and their age. We're going to be a pilot operation on this for the rest of the universities in this region.

Now we know that this is important information. We don't want to be hiring women administrators who are going to be getting pregnant soon and leaving us. We also know that women with pre-school-age children have higher absence rates than men. Also, we know that single women will soon be getting married and leaving the university either immediately or as their husbands are

258

transferred. Therefore, I'm asking each of you to note the women's marital status, age, and number of children during the employment interview.

Now we've got to be tactful about this. Don't come right out and ask them, but get at it in general conversation with the applicant. Make a note of it but keep it in a separate file from their application file. Mark it confidential. Don't even let the secretarial pool type up the information.

I know this all sounds secretive, but we've just got to have this information if we're going to make good hiring decisions.

Burt: Secretive, hell! It shounds illegal to me, Jack, I don't think we should do it.

Bob: Come on, now Burt. I think it's reasonable. We've just got to do this. It costs us a bundle each year because women leave to get married and have children.

Sally: Not all women do. We have many women who have been with our university for over twenty years.

Bob: Come on, Sally. We're not talking about secretaries and office clerks. We're talking about high-priced administrators.

Sally: Well, several of our women are administrative assistants making over $10,000 a year. I make more than that and I've been here for ten years.

Bob: Yeah, but you're fifty years old. You're stable. You won't be having any more kids or leaving to get married.

Sally: Bob, you're stereotyping. All young women aren't out to get married or have half a dozen kids. Let's just judge each individual on work potential, not on age, sex, marital status, or the number of children. Ours is the largest state university. We employ about 10,000 people, yet we have less than 1 percent women in top administrative jobs paying more than $35,000 a year. We ought to set a better example.

Jack: Hold on, hold on, Sally and Bob. You know we're trying to improve things. There are many things we're implementing like the talent bank and special recruiting and training programs for women. But we can't invest all these funds in young women and have them quit. We've got to recoup our investment. We've got to start running this operation more like a business and stop wasting the taxpayer's money. Now as head of personnel for this university, I'm asking each of you to start getting this information on the women you interview.

Sally: More like a business? O.K., then let's stop hiring these retired military types who come to us with their hard-lined military attitudes, stay a few years, do almost nothing, and then retire. Talk about wasting money! Think ot all these people who are already semiretired and who only stay a few years. We'd be better off replacing them with women who appreciate the opportunity and the challenge to manage. There are hundreds of women who would love some of these traditional male jobs and who would do a helluva better job.

Jack: So you're not going to go along with my suggestion, Sally?

Sally: No, I'm not. If the rest of you want to do it, fine. But I think it's clearly unethical and probably illegal.

Jack: O.K., Sally, what do you suggest we do? We just can't ignore the marriage problem. We want good women with administrative experience or potential, but we must have some assurance that they stay with us. What do you suggest?

259

2. Divide the class into groups of five to seven members. These groups are to discuss the preceding case, "In the Public Service?" assuming the role of the Midstate University Staff Affirmative Action Committee. This committee is in the process of developing a new affirmative action plan for nonfaculty staff for the university, and has just experienced the conversation that was described in the case. The following questions should be used to guide the group's discussion (*thirty minutes*):

    a. What are the major issues here?
    b. Is Jack's suggestion unethical and illegal as Sally maintains?
    c. What are the ramifications of implementing Jack's suggestion?
    d. What would you suggest if you were Sally? How would you go about dealing with this problem in this meeting?
    e. Is there a need to have some assurance of permanency from all people—male and female—before they are hired for a managerial position? How about before they are hired for a clerical position?
    f. Is Jack prejudiced? Is he operating on the basis of stereotypes?
    g. What would Jack's superior say if he knew of Jack's suggestion?
    h. What should the role of a large state university or other governmental agency be in promoting affirmative action and employment opportunities for women?

3. Each group should write what it thinks is the major problem (*fifteen minutes*).

4. Each group should list the first two steps it would take to deal with this problem (*fifteen minutes*).

5. Bring the small groups back together into the full class for discussion. The instructor should list on the board the problem statements and action steps from each group (*ten minutes*).

6. Discussion (*twenty minutes*).

C. Discussion and Conclusions

1. Is there any agreement among the groups as to the nature of the problem or what to do about it? What does this say about EEO problems and programs?

2. Would it be possible to develop a consensus on how to deal with these EEO problems? If not, what should an organization (its administrators and its policies) do?

3. What are the costs and benefits of:
   a. continuing to resist affirmative action efforts?
   b. developing an effective, even if not totally popular, affirmative action program?
   For each of these options, what would be the impact on recruiting, hiring, promotion, pay, job assignments, job descriptions and classifications, career planning, employee morale, supervisory morale?

4. What would be the result of an organizational policy which makes positive EEO results a mandatory part of an administrator's successful performance evaluation, tying pay and promotion at least partially to affirmative action results? Would there be any reason for doing this?

5. How can an agency or other governmental body make sure that both its personnel and its supervisory practices remain in line with legal, enforcement agency, and societal rules for discrimination in employment? Which of these takes precedence when there is disagreement?

D. Assessment of Learning

Think about what you have done in this exercise. Try to identify two or three major points that you have learned from this experience. What meaning do these points have for you as an individual and for you as an administrator? How might you put this learning to use outside the class?

Consider only what you have really learned. Don't try to figure out what other participants say they learned, or what you think you should have learned. If you feel you didn't learn anything, think about why. What could you have done to get more out of the exercise? How might the exercise have been structured differently to provide a better learning experience? What could be done in later exercises to help make them better learning experiences?

E.   lected Readings

1. Glueck, W.F., *Personnel: A Diagnostic Approach*, rev. ed. (Dallas: Business Publications, 1978), ch. 3, "Selection of personnel," and 18, "Equal employment opportunity programs."
2. Greenman, R.L., and Schmertz, E.J., *Personnel Administration and the Law*, 2d ed. (Washington, D.C.: The Bureau of National Affairs, 1979), ch. 3., "Equal employment opportunity and civil rights."
3. Hampton, R.E., "The response of governments and the Civil Service to anti-discrimination efforts," in L.J. Hausman, et al., eds., *Equal Rights and Industrial Relations* (Madison, Wis.: Industrial Relations Research Association, 1977).
4. Miner, M.G., and Miner, J.B., *Employee Selection Within the Law* (Washington, D.C.: The Bureau of National Affairs, 1978).
5. Nigro, F.A., and Nigro, L.G., *The New Public Personnel Administration* (Itasca, Ill.: F.E. Peacock Publishers, 1976), ch. 7, "Selection."
6. Stahl, O.G., *Public Personnel Administration*, 7th ed. (New York: Harper and Row, 1976), part 3, "Staffing."

EXERCISE 20

Employee Relations: Negotiating a Contract

Purpose

   1. To gain experience in the negotiation of collective bargaining contracts.
   2. To increase understanding of the purposes and tactics of successful employee relations.

Preparation

   Read the introduction.

Group Size

   Any size, in subgroups of ten to fifteen.

Time Requirement

   Ninety minutes.

Physical Setting

   Movable chairs and tables to simulate a negotiation situation.

Related Issues

   Group behavior, planning, goal setting, verbal and nonverbal communication, intergovernmental relations, budgeting, administrative responsibility.

263

A.   Introduction

Employee relations in the public sector increasingly involve collective negotiation of contracts between unions representing groups of employees and administrators representing government. Many special issues have arisen to complicate the nature of these negotiations. These issues range from a lack of controlling legislation to questions about who is management (the local administrator, the legislative body, the public)? Should private sector precedents and practices be followed? Or is the public sector somehow unique? If the nature of the relationship is different because neither side has the free recourse to tactics such as strikes or cessation of services, it is nevertheless true that the strategies and tactics of negotiation remain similar.

Both management and employee groups must consider and deal with the following types of questions. Furthermore, these issues provide the framework for effective negotiation, which has often been missing in the public sector because of the lack of experience and training of public sector negotiators.

1. What kind of preparation needs to be done and by whom?
    a. Research on economic data, employee interests, opponent's approach and position.
    b. Short- and long-term objectives to be accomplished through negotiations.
2. What type of negotiating team do you want or need?
    a. How large should it be?
    b. What knowledge and skills are desired?
3. What kind of contract do you want (very specific or general)?
4. How open (visible to the public) would you like the negotiations to be?
5. Who will actually do the negotiating (talking)? On which issues?
6. How much of your objectives and arguments do you want to disclose and when do you want to disclose it.
7. What type of image and posture do you wish to project? What has been the image and posture in the past (with what results)?
8. What expectations do you have (or would you like to create) for future negotiations?
9. What types of ritual and game playing do you and your opponents see as necessary?
    a. For support from respective constituencies?
    b. For the nature of your opening positions?
    c. For public (versus private) positions?
    d. For tactical purposes, such as trading and compromise?

10. Do you intend to build consensus on issues?
11. How much time do you have to negotiate a contract? How much time will be devoted to negotiation?

Dealing with these issues ahead of time can eliminate many of the difficulties often encountered by negotiators as a result of lack of experience or preparation. Richardson (1976) suggests the following guides for collective negotiations which produce results satisfactory to both sides:

1. Keep your real objectives confidential.
2. Don't hurry; when in doubt, caucus.
3. Be flexible; remember, bargaining is by nature compromise.
4. Try to understand why the other side is taking its position. Respect their need for face saving.
5. Build a reputation for firm but fair negotiating.
6. Control your emotions.
7. Measure each move against your objectives.
8. Remember, the impact of present concessions affects the future.

During the following exercise, you will be negotiating part of a contract between city workers and city government in a state with relatively liberal public sector collective bargaining statutes. While you are preparing for the negotiations, and during the negotiations themselves, keep in mind the above points. Upon completion of the exercise, you will be asked to examine the procedures that you followed, in an attempt to determine which procedures and tactics had what kinds of results.

B. Procedure

During this exercise you will be playing the role of either a city administrator on a city negotiating team, a city employee on a union negotiating team, or a state mediator. You will be negotiating a partial contract for the next two years. The city employees have been organized for eight years and this will be their fifth two-year contract. The first three negotiations broke down and ended in short employee strikes. Relationships between the city and its employees have not been particularly good and during the last year have gotten visibly worse, probably because of budget cutbacks and a few layoffs. Statewide, there has been strong pressure for limitations on property taxes, and there is currently a signature-gathering effort under way to get a measure on the fall ballot for such a purpose. It is predicted that such a measure, if approved by the voters—which is likely, would put further restrictions on the extent of services provided by city government. The inflation rate during the last year has been above the national average in this city. And the fast local growth in population is predicted to put continuing pressure on prices within the area.

The following are excerpts from the liberal state law governing collective bargaining among public employees in the state:

Collective bargaining is defined as: "The performance of the mutual obligation of a public employer and representative of its employees to (1) meet at reasonable times and (2) confer in good faith with respect to employment relations, or negotiation of agreement, or any question arising thereunder, and (3) the execution of a written contract incorporating any agreement reached if requested by either party."

Employment relations include, but not limited to, matters concerning direct and indirect monetary benefits, hours, vacations, sick leave, grievances and grievance procedures, and other conditions of employment.

If the parties cannot come to agreement, the law provides that they are to submit their differences to compulsory arbitration (a procedure which includes a preliminary fact-finding and mediation step prior to actual decision making by an arbitrator).

1. Divide the class into sets of three groups of approximately the following sizes: (a) management group, five to six persons; (b) union group, five to six persons; (c) mediator group, two to three persons. Each set of these groups will negotiate separate contracts based on the three issues on forms 1, 2, and 3 (*five minutes*).

2. Each group is to plan their negotiations over the three issues of wage increases, cost-of-living plan, and holiday package. The mediators should spend this planning time preparing their procedures for mediation, should they be called upon in an impasse. Forms 1, 2, and 3 present starting positions and potential ranges for settlement of these issues (*twenty minutes*).

3. Negotiate a settlement on the three issues, using forms 1, 2, and 3 as guides for positioning the final agreement (*thirty minutes*). (Mediators should observe negotiations during this time, but not participate.)

4. If agreement is not reached on all three issues at the end of the allotted thirty minutes, then the mediators have fifteen minutes to fact-find and try to mediate an agreement with the opposing sides (*fifteen minutes*).

5. Debriefing and discussion of negotiation outcomes (*at least twenty minutes*).

C. Discussion and Conclusions

1. What settlement(s) were reached?

2. What preparations were made by the different teams? What impact did those preparations have on the negotiations?

3. What tactics were used by the opposing sides during the negotiations? What impact did those tactics have?

4. What images were projected by the opposing sides? Did they influence the outcomes? In what way?

5. Are there procedures or tactics that either side didn't use but, if going through the exercise again, would now use? Why? Why weren't they used the first time? What does this say about real negotiations among real protagonists?

6. What techniques did the mediators use? With what effect? They suggest procedures that might make the original negotiations more effective?

D.   Assessment of Learning

Think about what you have done in this exercise. Try to identify two or three major points that you have learned from this experience. What meaning do these points have for you as an individual and for you as an administrator? How might you put this learning to use outside the class?

Consider only what you have really learned. Don't try to figure out what other participants say they learned, or what you think you should have learned. If you feel you didn't learn anything, think about why. What could you have done to get more out of the exercise? How might the exercise have been structured differently to provide a better learning experience? What could be done in later exercises to help make them better learning experiences?

E.   Selected Readings

Bunker, C., *Collective Bargaining: Nonprofit Sector* (Columbus, Ohio: Grid Publishing, 1975).

Hagburg, E.C., and Levine, M.J., *Labor Relations* (St. Paul, Minn.: West Publishing Co., 1978).

Hamermesh, D.S., ed., *Labor in the Public and Nonprofit Sectors* (Princeton, N.J.: Princeton University Press, 1975).

Nierenberg, G.I., *The Art of Negotiating* (New York: Hawthorne Books, 1968).

Richardson, R., "Positive collective bargaining," in D. Yoder and H.G. Heneman, Jr., eds., *Employee and Labor Relations*, ASPA Handbook of Personnel and Industrial Relations, vol. 3 (Washington, D.C.: Bureau of National Affairs, 1976).

Stahl, O.G., *Public Personnel Administration*, 7th ed. (New York: Harper and Row, 1976).

Stieber, J., *Public Employee Unionism: Structure, Growth, Policy* (Washington, D.C.: The Brookings Institute, 1973).

Walton, R.E., and McKersie, R.B., *A Behavioral Theory of Labor Negotiations* (New York: McGraw-Hill, 1965).

Weitzman, J., *The Scope of Bargaining in Public Employment* (New York: Praeger Publishers, 1975).

Wellington, H.H., and Winter, R.K., Jr., *The Unions and the Cities* (Washington, D.C.: The Brookings Institute, 1971).

Zagoria, S., ed., *Public Workers and Public Unions* (Englewood Cliffs, N.J.: Prentice-Hall, 1972).

F. Working Documents

Form 1

Wages

Union Points	1	2	3	4	5	6	7	8	9	10	11	12	13	14	15	16	17	18

Percentage Increase

	0	1	2	3	4	5	6	7	8	9	10	11	12	13	14	15	16	17

Management Points	18	17	16	15	14	13	12	11	10	9	8	7	6	5	4	3	2	1

Union demands 16 percent increase

Management offers 1 percent increase

Form 2

Cost-of-Living Clause

Union Points	1	2	3	4	5	6	7	8	9	10	11	12	13	14	15	16	17	18

Percentage of Cost-of-Living Increase Covered by Contract

5	10	15	20	25	30	35	40	45	50	55	60	65	70	75	80	85	90

Management Points	18	17	16	15	14	13	12	11	10	9	8	7	6	5	4	3	2	1

Union demands 85 percent Cost-of-Living Clause

Management offers 10 percent Cost-of-Living Clause

Form 3

Paid Holidays

| Union Points | 2 | 4 | 6 | 8 | 10 | 12 | 14 | 16 | 18 |

Number of Paid Holidays

| | 2 | 3 | 4 | 5 | 6 | 7 | 8 | 9 | 10 |
| Management Points | 18 | 16 | 14 | 12 | 10 | 8 | 6 | 4 | 2 |

Union demands nine paid holidays

Management offers three paid holidays

PART IV

Careers in Public Administration

PART IV   Careers in Public Administration

The last part of this book contains only one exercise, but that exercise is potentially one of the more important. The other exercises have stressed the development of skills, abilities, and knowledge necessary for the effective pursuit of the job of a public manager. This exercise, Self-Evaluation and Career Planning, on the other hand, stresses self-understanding and planning in order to increase the probability that the student will make the correct career choices, and thus be in a position to use these skills in an effective way. The skills make little difference if the individual is not in the right place at the right time to use them. This exercise is designed to increase the likelihood that this will happen.

Secondarily, the exercise also facilitates the student's analysis of his or her work-related strengths and weaknesses as well as his or her personal and work-related values. This self-understanding can improve considerably one's career preparation and choices. And that will greatly enhance one's likelihood of satisfaction with his or her job.

EXERCISE 21
Self-Evaluation and Career Planning

Purpose

1. To develop an understanding of the concept of careers.
2. To develop skills in career planning.
3. To provide an appreciation of the difficulties associated with career planning in public service.
4. To increase the likelihood of career success.

Preparation

Read the introduction and do step 1 of the procedure.

Group Size

Any size (broken into small groups of three to five members).

Time Requirement

Ninety minutes.

Physical Setting

Movable chairs or facilities for small groups to meet without disturbing other groups.

Related Issues

Goal setting, time management, self-analysis, planning.

273

A.   Introduction

Most people spend most of their adult waking lives at work. Typically, the single most important and time-consuming adult activity, the major source of income, and the major arena for exhibiting and developing our skills and competence is the world of work. It should be no surprise that the world of work provides social status and personal identity for many people. This is particularly true for people who work for government because of their commitments to public service.

Even though work plays such a central role in individual lives and self-concepts, the sequence of work experiences over a lifetime—their career—often "just happens." Many people sense little control or choice in their careers. They make career decisions with little care or thought, little appreciation of the implications of their decisions, little recognition of the relationships between their decisions. Yet feelings of personal success and personal satisfaction, particularly related to work and careers, require self-selected goals, challenge, growth, and autonomy as well as accomplishment.

At the same time that increasing numbers of persons are becoming interested in how to enhance their career successes, organizations are also becoming concerned about issues related to career success. The need to improve opportunities for women and minorities, scarcity of competent managers, high levels of dissatisfaction and resultant turnover and lack of work commitment are all reasons why organizations are becoming involved with career development and planning.

People who study careers have typically separated into two camps: the differentialists and the developmentalists. The differentialists have studied careers in terms of identifiable individual differences in personalities, abilities, backgrounds, and work values. They have viewed career success as congruence between these individual characteristics and organizational requirements.

Among the more productive of these approaches has been the focus on work orientations or values which are presumed to develop over time from a person's "success experiences." That is, people develop career interests based on what they are good at and their feelings of career satisfaction and based on their working in jobs which are congruent with these values. As Holland (1973) and Schein (1975) have shown (see figure 21.1), people develop fairly stable and identifiable interests related to desired occupations.

The developmentalists, on the other hand, have studied careers in terms of fairly standard developmental stages through which people go as they make career choices, implement theory, and move toward occu-

```
┌──────────────────────────────────────────────────────────────┐
│                                                                │
│            Occupation Categories (Holland 1973)                │
│                                                                │
│     Category                    Focus of Interest              │
│                                                                │
│  1. Realistic:  skilled or technical work                      │
│  2. Investigative:  service or research activities             │
│  3. Artistic:  creative (words, music, art)                    │
│  4. Social:  work with people (healing, helping, teaching)     │
│  5. Enterprising:  persuasion (sales, politics, merchandising) │
│  6. Conventional:  office jobs (working with organizations,    │
│                    files, regular schedules)                   │
│                                                                │
└──────────────────────────────────────────────────────────────┘
```

```
┌──────────────────────────────────────────────────────────────┐
│                                                                │
│              Career Anchors (Schein 1975)                      │
│                                                                │
│     Value                       Focus of Interest              │
│                                                                │
│  1. Managerial competence:  opportunities to manage (involves  │
│                    interpersonal competence, analytical        │
│                    competence, emotional stability, the        │
│                    "will to manage")                           │
│  2. Technical/functional competence:  technical expertise      │
│  3. Security:  stability in organizations or geographic area   │
│  4. Creativity:  create something you can call your own        │
│  5. Autonomy and independence:  being free of organizational   │
│                    constraints                                 │
│                                                                │
└──────────────────────────────────────────────────────────────┘
```

FIGURE 21.1   Occupational and Career Interests

pational maturity. Figure 21.2 summarizes the models of a number of developmentalists. In each model, the presumption for career success is that individuals must complete certain activities related to career decisions before moving on to the next stage.

The challenge to many developmentalists, as well as to the differentialists, is to keep the individual on a growth curve at middle age and retirement, rather than mere maintenance or decline. Career strategists identify two important components to ongoing individual career development. This exercise tries to focus on both components.

The first component of career growth is planning. Planning includes the need to know yourself, your interests, values, strengths, and weaknesses. It includes knowing your situation and as much as possible about your options. And it includes preparation: setting goals, prioriti-

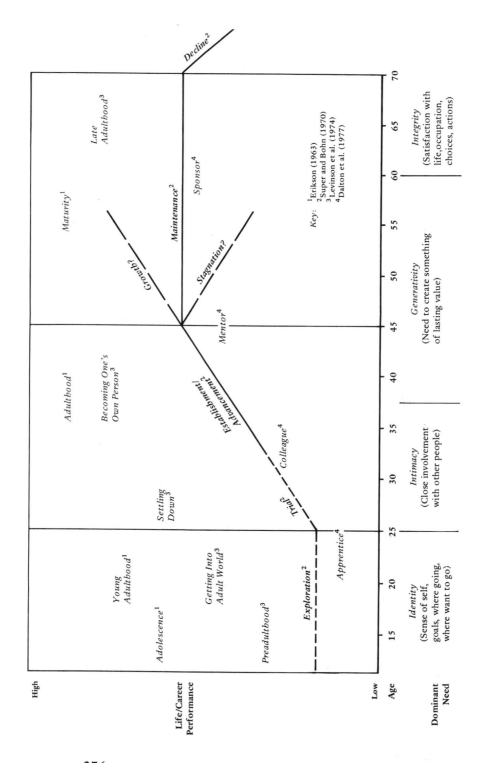

Figure 21.2 An Integrative Model of Life and Career Stages (*Source: Adapted from D. T. Hall, Careers in Organizations.* (*Santa Monica, Calif.: Goodyear Publishing Company, 1976), p. 57. Adapted with permission of the publisher.*)

276

zing them, developing action plans for achieving those goals, and creating checkpoints and timetables for accomplishment.

The second component of career growth is an appreciation of the importance of job assignments. Most personal growth for adults occurs on and through the job. But for job assignments to be developmental, they must involve some stretch. That is, if people are only performing activities that they have already mastered, there will be no growth or development. Thus people must seek challenging assignments that will develop the skills and abilities identified in the planning stage as necessary for the achievement of their goals.

To this general discussion of career development must be added some comments about careers in government. Mobility in government jobs at all levels (local, state, and federal) has generally been restricted to within-agency movement. This, coupled with the normally confining and highly structured job classification systems now in use in government, often limits the opportunities for advancement, to say nothing of the chances for seeking and using job assignments in a planned and developmental way. But this is gradually changing. More and more there is movement among levels of government, between agencies, and from private and nonprofit to government and vice versa. These types of movement should make it easier for civil servants to adequately plan their own careers and enhance their possibilities for career success and satisfaction.

The following exercise provides a mechanism for analyzing one's self, related to career, and to begin the task of career planning. It involves both individual and group actions. In these activities, as is also true elsewhere, the more you put into the exercise, the more you will get out. In career planning the stakes are high, but the rewards are more than worth the effort.

B.   Procedure*

1.   Prior to class, perform the following steps:

    a.   For each of these three areas—relationships and affiliations, personal fulfillment (however you define it), and career—draw a business progress chart that depicts your past, present, and future. On the progress line, mark an X to show where you are now. An example of such business progress charts is given in figure 21.3.

*This exercise is adapted from Pfeiffer, J.M., and Jones, J.E. (Eds.), *A Handbook of Structured Experiences for Human Relations Training*, Vol. II, Rev. (La Jolla, CA: University Associates, 1974). Used with permission.

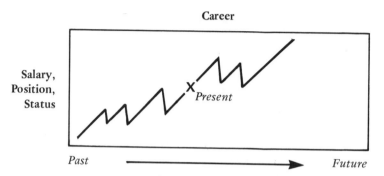

FIGURE 21.3   *Sample Business Progress Chart*

b. For each of the three areas (relationships, personal fulfillment, career), make a list of ten adjectives or traits which describe you with regard to that area. Mark each of these traits or attributes as + (positive), − (negative), or 0 (neutral), based on how you feel about it.

c. For each of these three areas, develop up to five personal goals you have for where you would like to be in each of these. List your ideal attainments. Be as free as possible in selecting your goals. Mark each of these goals as:
    1. of little importance
    2. of moderate importance
    3. of great importance
    4. of very great importance

d. Combine your list of goals into one list of fifteen goals. This list should reflect the relative importance you place on these goals, that is, it should reflect how you think the goals from the separate lists relate to each other, with the most important goals at the top of the list.

e. Choose the most important goal from this list from each of the three areas: relationships, personal fulfillment, and career. Write a statement describing what you would like to be doing one year from today in order to be moving toward achievement of each of those three goals. In the case of the career goal, this should be a job description, identifying the job you would like to hold one year from now as you move toward achievement of your major career goal.

2. In class, form into groups of three to five people (*five minutes*).

3. Each person should choose one of their important career goals for discussion in the group. As a group, help each other develop an

action plan for achievement of the individual's career goal and/or job as described in step e, above. This action plan should include specific steps to be taken, the expected outcomes, and deadlines for their achievement, with assignment of specific responsibilities by the individual for the accomplishment of each step in the action plan.

The most effective use of the group can be made if each member comes to the group prepared with or seeking the answers to these questions (*sixty minutes*):

a.   Is this goal realistic?

b.   What will happen if I don't achieve it?

c.   What are my strengths and weaknesses that affect my ability to achieve this goal?

d.   What obstacles will prevent me from achieving this goal?

e.   Which of my personal values are addressed by this goal?

f.   When do I realistically hope to achieve this goal?

g.   What am I overlooking? What is likely to go wrong?

4.   Discussion (*twenty-five minutes*).

C.   Discussion and Conclusions

1.   Is career planning more difficult in the public sector than in the private sector? Why?

2.   Who has responsibility for career planning: the individual? the agency? the supervisor? the personnel administrator? nobody? Why? What difference does it make who does it?

3.   Why is it important to know both yourself and your options?

4.   Why is it helpful (some would say necessary) to make a public commitment to your career goals and to develop a support group to help and encourage you in your pursuit of those goals?

D.   Assessment of Learning

Think about what you have done in this exercise. Try to identify two or three major points that you have learned from this experience. What meaning do these points have for you as an individual and for you as an administrator? How might you put this learning to use outside the class?

Consider only what you have really learned. Don't try to figure out what other participants say they learned, or what you think you should have learned. If you feel you didn't learn anything, think about why. What could you have done to get more out of the exercise? How might the exercise have been structured differently to provide a better learning experience? What could be done in later exercises to help make them better learning experiences?

E.   Selected Readings

Bolles, R.N., *What Color is Your Parachute?* (Berkeley, Calif.:   Ten Speed Press, 1979).

Bray, D.W., Campbell, R.J., and Grant, D.L., *Formative Years in Business* (New York: John Wiley and Sons, 1974).

Dalton, G.W., Thompson, P.H., and Price, R., "Career stages: a model of professional careers in organizations," *Organizational Dynamics* (Summer 1977), 19–42.

Erikson, E.H., *Childhood and Society*, New York: Norton, 1963.

Hall, D.T., *Careers in Organizations* (Santa Monica, Calif.:   Goodyear Publishing, 1976).

Hall, F.S. and Hall, D.T., *The Two-Career Couple* (Reading, Mass.:   Addison-Wesley, 1979).

Holland, J.L., *Making Vocational Choices: A Theory of Careers* (Englewood Cliffs, N.J.:   Prentice-Hall, 1973).

Jelinek, M., ed., *Career Management for the Individual and the Organization* (Chicago: St. Clair Press, 1979).

Levinson, D.J., Darrow, Klein, E., Levinson, M., McKee, B., "The psychological development of men in early adulthood and the mid-life transition," in D.F. Hicks, A. Thomas, and M. Roff, eds., *Life History Research in Psychopathology*, vol. 3 (Minneapolis: University of Minnesota Press, 1974).

Miller, D.B., *Personal Vitality* (Reading, Mass.:   Addison-Wesley, 1977).

Nigro, F.A. and Nigro, L.G., *The New Public Personnel Administration* (Itasca, Ill.: F.E. Peacock, 1976), ch. 4, "Careers and the structure of the service," and 8, "Career management."

Pursely, R., and Snortland, N., *Managing Government Organizations* (North Scituate, Mass.: Duxbury Press, 1980), ch. 8, "New issues in public personnel management."

Schein, E.W., "How career anchors hold executives to their career paths," *Personnel*, 52, 3(1975), 11–24.

Sheehy, G., *Passages* (New York: Dutton, 1976).

Sperry, L., Mickelson, D.J., and Hunsaker, P.L., *You Can Make it Happen* (Reading, Mass.: Addison-Wesley, 1977).

Stahl, O.G., *Public Personnel Administration*, 7th ed. (New York: Harper and Row, 1976), ch. 4, "Career systems," and 5, "Classification of positions."

Super, D.E., and Bohn, M.J., Jr., *Occupational Psychology* (Belmont, Calif.: Wadsworth, 1970).

APPENDIX A

Group Formation

Groups can be formed in many ways. The method chosen is mostly determined by whether the groups are to remain together for an extended period of time or whether they will change their memberships with each exercise. If the memberships are to change frequently, the method chosen is not so critical. Counting off by the size of the group, letting class members choose their own groups, arbitrarily splitting the class into required group size using natural breaks—all will work about equally well. Obviously, counting off tends to break up groups that have already chosen to be sitting together. This may have the advantages of breaking up cliques and letting persons be freer to try new roles. But it also mandates the use of additional time for group members to get to know each other so that they can interact more effectively. Using frequently changing memberships may require class members to develop techniques for getting acquainted early in the life of a group. Purposely working at getting acquainted can greatly enhance the effectiveness of a group.

If group membership is to stay the same for a longer period of time, it may seem appropriate to try to balance the memberships of the groups along skill, education, experience, age, or other criteria. Here, class members might begin their participation by trying to develop a consensus on the issue of relatively permanent groups (perhaps changed once or twice during a term) versus constantly changing groups and on the issue of which criteria are important, if any, for formation of the initial groups. Extended-life groups are obviously necessary for projects that are handled over the length of the course or outside of class. And they provide greater opportunity for the development of interpersonal relations that allow more openness and trust, so important to the effective interaction required by learning through exercises.

This is a quick introduction to the topic of group formation. Table A.1 summarizes the pros and cons of the different options. This should help the teacher who is new to experiential learning with one of the early and important issues of the use of group activities for learning.

TABLE A.1   *Advantages and Disadvantages of Various Options for Group Formation*

Frequent Change	Extended Membership
Pros	
Meet many people	Chance to develop openness and trust through longer relationships; greater knowledge about each other
Exposed to more variance in background, knowledge	Less time required (except initially) to get acquainted
More chances for members to try on new group roles	Necessary for long-term projects
Better for groups of people who already know each other	May be better for development of team-building and group skills
Cons	
Difficult to develop trust, openness that comes from longer-term relationships	Group expectations of individual behavior patterns can lock members into perhaps undesired (by them) roles
Additional time required at each exercise for getting acquainted	Cliques can develop
	Persons can get stuck in perhaps undesirable (by groups) roles
	Greater chance for dysfunctional group norms to develop

APPENDIX B
Group Role Plays

Organizations achieve their goals through group and individual efforts. Increasingly, these efforts are group efforts. Tasks and objectives require ever increasing levels of coordination and interdependence. Relationships proliferate and interactions between individuals and groups compound the complexities of assignments. Mediating conflict, coordinating diverse interests, and facilitating group processes have become major aspects of every administrator's job.

This discussion outlines a few of the issues that administrators must consider when performing their roles in today's organizations. It does not provide an in-depth discussion of issues and processes.

Group Behavior

How effectively a group performs is dependent upon two aspects of group behavior: (1) its efforts toward completing the task(s) it was assigned; and (2) the extent to which the individual members of the group find it sufficiently rewarding and interesting to continue working with the other members of the group in completing its task. The roles created by these two aspects of group behavior are constantly being played by different persons within a group situation. There are several roles involved, and they can be addressed best by a variety of people.

Group effectiveness is also influenced by its members' abilities to recognize behaviors that inhibit, deflect, or stop its progress toward the accomplishment of its tasks, achievement of its goals, maintenance of beneficial work relations among members, and the meeting of the individual needs of the group's members. Effective groups can solve these problems with the minimum amount of energy and disturbance.

Some of the common problems encountered by work groups are as follows:

1. *Hidden agendas*
   People's behavior is the result of many forces, some of which are external to the group situation. Persons often have goals or aspira-

tions that influence their actions but that they are not willing to explain to others. These hidden agendas often lead individuals to obscure their real thoughts and feelings from the rest of the group. This can hamper group interaction and decision making.

2. *Goal distortion*

Lack of group progress toward a goal may be the result of the group members' perceptions of that goal. Goals are often unclear or appear contradictory to group members. This too hampers group progress toward its objectives.

3. *Conflict*

All groups incorporate conflicts among differing points of view. Unless the group knows how to use these differences constructively to improve its information, decision making can be stymied or become a stilted, uncreative process.

4. *Breakdowns in communication*

Group ineffectiveness can result from breakdowns in either the sending or receiving of communications. Such breakdowns can be caused by language barriers resulting from different cultures, special jargon particular to an occupation, poor listening or speaking skills, or stereotyping people and filtering what they say throught the stereotype. Removal of these blocks requires concerted efforts by the group's leader (administrator) and by its members. It must be a shared responsibility and takes considerable time and effort. Often an outside impartial observer or consultant is necessary to facilitate group learning processes in these regards.

Group Leadership

Leadership is critical to the success of most groups. The demands of the organization and task, the needs of the members of the group, and the needs of the leader all influence which leadership style is appropriate or will be effective. Leadership styles can range from very autocratic, task-oriented styles to highly participative or delegative styles, with many combinations in between. Each style can be effective in the proper situation. The leader needs to monitor the situation and to match a style to the circumstances. A mature group, one that can set and achieve its own goals, will probably have a high degree of shared responsibility for leadership and decision making.

Group Decision Making

A number of considerations are important to a group and its leader for facilitating effective decision making. Among these are the following:

286

1. *The quality of the decision itself*

   How important is it that the decision be a quality decision? Important decisions require the input of quality information as well as the participation of persons with that information. The generation of many alternate solutions can also be necessary for quality decision making. If the decision is less critical, fewer resources and less time need to be committed to it.

2. *The acceptance of the decision by the relevant parties involved*

   Once the decision is made, will it be accepted by all who have to work with that decision? Administrators should make sure that decisions will be acceptable to and have the support of the people in key positions of the organization. Generally, this means that these key people need to be involved in the decision-making process itself.

3. *Speed of the decision*

   The decision-making process should take time into account. Some decisions are needed on a rush basis. Will those making the decisions be able to cope with this? Will the quality of the decision be lowered because of the time constraints? If time is critical, group decision making may be ruled out because of the length of time normally required for completion.

4. *Values used in the decision process*

   It is important to remember that all decisions are value decisions, that is, they determine what is good or bad, important or unimportant about the outcomes of the decision. Administrators must decide whose values should be considered in the decision-making process: their own, their organization's, or others'.

5. *Cost of the decision process*

   Decision making costs organizational resources, including the time of the people involved in the decision process. There is a relationship between the amount of resources spent and the quality, speed, and acceptance of decisions. Managers must identify and evaluate these costs and their payoffs.

Group effectiveness, group leadership, group decision making—all involve processes that influence how well a group or an organization accomplishes its objectives. Additionally, all of these processes are further complicated by the political games that persons and groups play in order to promote their own self-interests in any given situation or decision.

The administrator must try to make order out of the chaos and to accomplish personal and organizational objectives. It is not easy. It is often frustrating and stressful. But success requires the effort.

Selected Readings

Bradford, L.P., *Making Meetings Work* (La Jolla, Calif.: University Associates, 1976).

Maier, N.R.F., Solem, A.R., and Maier, A.A., *The Role-Play Technique* (La Jolla, Calif.: University Associates, 1975).

Napier, R.W., and Gershenfeld, M.K., *Groups: Theory and Practice* (Boston: Houghton Mifflin, 1973).

Schein, E.H., *Process Consultation: Its Role In Organization Development* (Reading, Mass.: Addison-Wesley, 1969).

Towers, J.M., *Role-Playing for Managers* (Oxford: Pergammon Press, 1974).

APPENDIX C

Background Information on CETA

A. Employment and Training Programs Prior to CETA

Beginning in the early 1960s, Congress enacted several programs to provide unemployed, underemployed, and economically disadvantaged workers with the assistance needed to be able to compete for, secure, and hold jobs successfully. These employment and training programs generally provide the following services: counseling, testing, job skills training in the classroom or on the job, basic or remedial education, work experience, job development, and placement. They often include supportive services such as child care, health care, and transportation; and many include job restructuring or job creation in public service employment.

Prior to the enactment of the Comprehensive Employment and Training Act (CETA), most of these services were provided under a variety of piecemeal and poorly coordinated federal laws. The planning and design of pre-CETA employment and training programs were carried out at the federal level: Service delivery on the local level was hampered by restrictive, federally-imposed program regulations which defined target groups who could only be served in extremely narrow categorical terms and allowed no flexibility in program design to adapt to local economic conditions.

B. Overview of CETA Legislation

The Comprehensive Employment and Training Act, enacted in December 1973, consolidated federally funded employment and training programs and allowed local elected officials to have more voice in planning and managing programs operating within their jurisdictions. CETA replaced and streamlined the previous array of separately funded, federally designed and administered categorical employment and training programs with a more flexible, decentralized, locally responsive system.

Adapted from *Access to Jobs: 1977 Annual Report* (Salem, Oreg.: Mid-Willamette Valley Manpower Consortium, 1977). Reprinted by permission.

Under CETA, the elected officials of local governments with populations in excess of 100,000 are eligible to be designated as prime sponsors through the Department of Labor according to a specified formula based on local unemployment rates and other factors. Within broad federal guidelines, prime sponsors have considerable latitude in defining specific target groups to be served, determining employment and training services to be provided, and deciding how and by whom those services should be delivered. Two or more prime sponsors can join together to form a consortium.

The governor serves as prime sponsor for all areas within a state which do not have any other level of government serving a population in excess of 100,000. At their discretion, however, these smaller local governments can join other prime sponsors to form consortia. Those that remain under the governor's direction form the balance-of-state prime sponsorship.

C.   Employment and Training Activities and Services

Employability development activities and services cover a wide range of assistance that can be classified into three major categories: (1) employment and training services, (2) employment and training program activities, and (3) supportive services. The following is an explanation of these activities and services within these categories:

1. Employment and Training Services:
   Recruiting eligible CETA applicants
   Determining each applicant's minimum financial needs for economic self-sufficiency
   Assessing specific developmental assistance needed by the applicant to be able to secure a job meeting minimum financial needs
   Determining whether the specific services can be feasibly delivered within the capabilities of the CETA programs
   Designing and implementing a plan of action to provide those services
   Assisting the participant to secure appropriate unsubsidized employment upon program completion
2. Employment and Training Program Activities:
   Classroom vocational training
   Work experience
   On-the-job training

Public service employment (temporary subsidized jobs in public agencies and private nonprofit organizations)

3. Supportive Services. Allows the provision of various services necessary to enable a specific participant to participate successfully in CETA activities. Supportive services include but are not limited to the following:

Transportation assistance. Allowances paid or other provisions made for commuting to and from the participant's home and the training site.

Child care assistance. Allowances to ensure proper care of children while the parent participates in a CETA program.

Health care. Service provided to identify and correct physical, mental, and dental deficiencies when no other resources are available.

Legal assistance. Provides referrals to legal services.

Emergency aid. Assistance provided to participants in the form of money or goods on a one-time basis for an emergency.

Bonding. Provides bonds to allow ex-offenders to work for employers who may require such assurance.

Housing assistance. Provides assistance in locating housing in proximity to the training or work site and financial assistance for moving, deposits, etc.

Clothing/uniforms. Provides assistance in obtaining clothing, uniforms, shoes, etc., needed to participate in training or a job.

D. Source of Funding

The funding for the Comprehensive Employment and Training Act is appropriated by Congress from federal tax monies and administered by the U.S. Department of Labor/Employment and Training Administration through ten regional offices. The funds are allocated on a fiscal grant basis among locally designated prime sponsors in accordance with formulas specified in the legislation. The amount received by each prime sponsor is determined by the formula written into the law, although a small percentage of the total funds available can be distributed by the secretary of labor without reference to the formula.

E. The CETA Office

Although elected officials (mayors, county commissioners, governors) are designated as the prime sponsors, the work of planning and implementing local employment and training programs is done by professional staff hired for that purpose. In some localities this staff, the local CETA office, is primarily involved in planning, and contracts with other agencies to provide program services. In other localities CETA offices have very large staffs and are involved in providing services directly to program participants. In all cases there is a ceiling on how much of an area's CETA grant can be spent on administrative costs.